I'LL FIX AMERICA TONIGHT

(WELL, AT LEAST BY THE WEEKEND)

NATHAN ANDREW ROBERTS

I'll Fix America Tonight
(well, at least by the weekend)
All Rights Reserved.
Copyright © 2020 Nathan Andrew Roberts
v4.0

Outskirts Press, Inc.
http://www.outskirtspress.com

ISBN: 978-1-9772-2273-2

PRINTED IN THE UNITED STATES OF AMERICA

Table of Contents

Introduction

REVOLUTIONS START WITH revolutionary ideas.
Whether violent or peaceful, justified or wicked, successful or disastrous, they all start with ideas. Ideas
begin with someone who desperately wants to make
a change. Not in the hearts in minds of others, but in
their own. Sometimes revolutions result in the peaceful overthrow of an oppressive regime and sometimes
they result in a monarch's family being murdered in
the street. Sometimes they result in society changing
as a whole, sometimes in society snapping back to being even more guarded than before. Sometimes they
result in positive change for everyone, sometimes increased suffering. Whatever shape, form, timeframe,
and result they take, they all start with ideas.

What we need is a revolution. Peaceful of course.
It has to be said. There are a lot of people danger-
ously treading the boundary of violent uprising. I've
got a few revolutionary ideas. I've changed myself for
the better over the years and I hope to help others

do the same. If not, at least give them a few hours' distraction.

This book is intended as a suggestion for positive change collectively through some lessons learned anecdotally and a lifelong study of humanity. The direction of my life has been affected by many factors. Although the suffering I've endured may have been due to my horrible decision making skills and impulsive actions taken following peyote-infused vision quests, I am an American and that means not taking full (or even partial) responsibility for my problems. Due to this, I think the most impactful event for me was that owl I hit driving home to Flint, MI late at night on I-75 during my one year of studies at Wayne State University in Detroit, MI. I make many, many jokes in this book, but this isn't even one. I actually hit an owl on the expressway in 1999. Having done my most meaningful learning from movies and YA fantasy literature, I know of a certainty that owls are powerfully magical creatures. They probably also have a healthy and vibrant grapevine and I have no doubt they all quickly learned of Phil's (he looked like a Phil) ignoble death. So what we have here is basically the curse equivalent of offending a gypsy while erecting a condo development on an Indian burial ground while drunkenly inviting a coven (Gaggle? Flock? Herd? Murder?) of vampires into one's house.

Now, there are some ideas pertaining to a lot of facets of our society contained herein. What I would ask of even the most unreasonable of readers is that if you detest one idea or belief of mine that you refrain from waving off all others. That's just petty. This book is a buffet. Even people who pick the meat out the greens at the buffet line—along with those who scold them for being so obnoxiously picky—can't say they've had an entirely unpleasant experience at the restaurant.

Government (including education and municipalities), business, places of worship, and other societal groupings are the pillars of society. Family is the foundation. When the foundation crumbles, so do the pillars. What I propose is drastic changes to all of these. Mind you, many of my ideas come from a morally conservative Christian viewpoint (if you can't even bear to listen to my words past this sentence, I would be happy to provide you a refund) but I take a centrist and liberal stance on many different political and societal issues. I intend to put forth ideas that might work for everyone. I'll try to spare everyone lengthy preachiness espousing my worldview. As a Christian, I see evangelism and bringing glory to God as the meaning to my life. While I intend to glorify God with the words of this book, I don't intend it to be an evangelistic book. Other, wiser, smarter Christian men in corduroy jackets adorned with leather elbow patches have put enough ink to paper on that topic if you're looking for answers. I believe everyone (everyone? Yes EVERYONE) can work together. Writing a book listing your beliefs and then criticizing others who don't share your core values for not living up to your beliefs is like shooting dead fish in a drained barrel. I intend to do something much more difficult, but rewarding. Fix America. I'm no hero. Only one man (hands on hips, head tilted to the right and up, cape flowing in the wind, posing too long for it not to be weird, apparently with no particular place to go).

Liberals have some good ideas. And some bad ones. Sometimes they execute them well, sometimes disastrously. Conservatives have some good ideas. And some bad ones. Sometimes they execute them well, sometimes disastrously. I have found that drawing your support for politicians down party lines is foolish. I have also found that party line politicians will do quite a lot to ascertain, maintain, and grow their power. I address this in the following chapter. Speaking of which, let's get right into it. Lengthy introductory chapters are self-serving and redundant.

Government

Fear

Fear induces action. It makes people give power to those who promise to protect them from whatever danger they've enumerated and vowed to counteract. Democrats want us to fear. Republicans want us to fear. Every few years, they are able to get us to fear enough give some new guy the chance to change his address to 1600 Pennsylvania Ave. It's not as simplistic as that, but fear is definitely a factor. It's what I call the Fear Factor (copyright pending...wait, what? Already taken!? Raspberries!)

What do they want us to fear? I'm glad you asked. I didn't vote republican in the last few elections, but many of them are my ideological cousins and step-cousins, twice removed. As a moral conservative, I won't claim to be republican because many of them aren't morally conservative. Anyway, I'll start with my family first. Never let it be said that I'll kick every dog but my own. Republicans want us to fear the big T.

Terrorism. 9/11. Needle abruptly removed from record. Scratching noise. Awkward silence. Everyone pull in a collective gasp. Do the double head turn and make sure there are no Musselmen around. Look to the heavens and repeat the mantra "Never forget". In the next hour or so, hit the normal talking points about Sharia Law, Shiites vs. Sunnis (coming to Pay-Per-View in March), the crusades, beheadings, how their ideology is mutually exclusive with western values, and then give me one big whopping super-sized break. With fries and a Mountain Dew (no ice).

The Muslims of the world who raise families, start businesses, and live in peace outnumber the radicals, who, due to our diligence, have mostly stayed in their home countries. I'm not Catholic but understand that in non-Christian eyes, the historical evils of the Catholic church are lumped in with the rest of Christianity. Radical Jihadist Muslims have long memories and still refer to England, France, and other European countries as crusading countries. Constant interference (might I say needless since we have and utilize our own oil reserves now) by a country founded on Judeo-Christian principles in the Middle East has, in the minds of the radicals, been seen as a continuation of the Crusades. I'm not saying it's fair or right, I'm saying it's reality. Like Rand Paul, I fiercely advocate for a measured step back, asking that the people of the Muslim and Arab world to blossom where they are planted without American interference. The unfortunate thing for Rand Paul is that many staunch republicans advocate for fierce influence on our part in Asia Minor.

Republicans who constantly tout the threat of terrorism as the reason for their deserving power are being disingenuous. And their policing of the Arab world hasn't done much to quell the problem either. We aren't here to solve the problems of the Old World. One could make the argument that if we start leaving them alone, rates of terrorism would drop. Dubya misspoke when he stated they hate us for our freedoms. They don't. They hate us for our decadence and excesses. Remember when I said it's foolish to criticize those not of your worldview and theology for not living up to your morality? That's exactly what unreasonable Muslims do. They want freedom themselves within the bounds of their morality and it's idiotic to think they hate us for ours. They also hate us for our interference. Remove at least that one and the hatred might cool. There's a difference between diligence and nation-building in geopolitical quagmires that don't share our democratic values. I suggest the warmongering and warhawking republican party ponder the difference for a spell.

Now, am I saying that terrorism isn't real? Nope. Am I denigrating the memory of our greatest national disaster? I hope not. Much of what I write in this book is from a satirist viewpoint, so please take it in that spirit. I remember almost every second of 9/11/2001, but I'm afraid we went a bridge too far after that. What am I saying? Since our tightening of security and undying vigilance in response to that day, it's not close enough to home for us to blindly give power to an entire political party completely willing to alienate, ostracize, and anger the world's second largest religion. And since predicting all terrorism is impossible, we should be diligent in the ways we know how, limiting our interference, and bringing to justice those who commit it when they do. It's not perfect but it's the best one can do with an enemy who doesn't fight by the old rules of war.

Where is home? For me, it's the north suuiiide of Flint, Michigan (Beecher district). My area is quite poor. We've got two housing projects. When I lived in the actual city of Flint I had the water as a point of concern. I pay exorbitant insurance rates for my car because other folks in my city have shown a track record of taking others' stuff. Bandos in my city are often burned down on Devil's Night. I take my kids to a hotel in the suburbs on New Year's Eve because shooting guns into the air is accepted as a worthy way to ring in the new year. Blight peppers the city to the point that if I were coming out of living in an underground bunker for thirty years, I'd think that plywood windows were a popular decorative choice. We have few police and a city government plagued by corruption. In the top ten violent cities most years. When we aren't number one, I've considered walking around beating people up because if you're not first, you're last. For the love of Pete, we have a Netflix documentary showing outsiders how jacked up our city is. I don't know how many times I said "HEY! I know that place!" while watching it. Terrorists don't target Flint, Michigan. We've done a good enough job messing it up ourselves. I've got bills to pay. Through the school year 2017-2018, I taught in Pontiac, MI (Flint 2.0 as I call it) in a tiny charter school system and delivered pizza at night. I recently looked into buying a pistol and getting my CPL because, surprise surprise, the bad guys have guns and they target pizza delivery drivers.

Point is, terrorism is real, just not as real as things I see every day. I would argue that it's the same for most Americans. Here in Flint and the greater Detroit Metro area we have wealthy suburbs like Grand Blanc, Birmingham, Royal Oak, Grosse Pointe Shores, and Beverly Hills. Los Angeles has its own Beverly Hills (possibly a bit more famous than the one here). Many folks living there aren't in touch with big urban city problems, nor the problems associated with poor rural area problems. It's the grass roots constituency of rural republicans who allowed Trump to change his address, moving from one big house to another one. But are republican leaders talking about fixing the urban areas? No, they are busy dissing democrats for messing them up. Really? You guys don't have anything to do with it? Oh, you were serious? Ok, while we're telling tales, I'm 6'6" and am deadly beyond the three-point line in the clutch. Average minds criticize. Good minds offer solutions. What's that? Black and Spanish people don't vote for you and they make up the majority of people in big cities? I see. So they can only get help once they start voting for you? Priorities.

Crime, a failing education system, widespread acceptance of mediocrity, laughably misplaced hyper-confidence, generational poverty, and the breakdown of the family are hurting America more. Terrorism is real, just not all that often, and less a threat than those others. Call crime homeland terrorism if that's what you need to justify turning your money, attention, and efforts on it. Our CIA and government are so caught up in spending obscene amounts of money policing the world, they forget the home front. More on this later.

You're not off the hook on this one, democrats.

What do they want us to fear? Perpetual winter...I mean global warming...I mean massive draught...I mean devastating flood...actually it's polar vortexes shifting their circumferential gravimetric dramalan-gitude...Heavens to Murgatroyd, I mean climate change...I meant global warming all along...except for when I don't mean that. In that case, see one of the others I mentioned, whichever one applies to the situation and helps me win the argument. Their prog-nostication of what's going to happen to the world has been updated, pivoted, and overhauled altogether nearly as many times as the theory of evolution.

I don't care to settle the science here because I'm not capable. There's also the matter that scientists haven't settled it. They do tend to disagree. That "97% of scientists" thing was a hoax because it was 97% of those polled. It's not hard to manipulate numbers to your advantage. Science and evidence can be bent to your biases and whoever is supplying your research grant. Climate change is real and has always been real since like, forever. Our world is ever-changing. We've had warm and cold spells. Since nerds have started tracking the temperature, we've warmed up a whole two degrees. If we are contributing to problems, awesome. Let's change things. Starting with you guys. Start burning candles, stop flying in jets, give your palatial houses to multiple families who would have to walk half a mile to interact with each other on the inside of the house, don't buy or consume anything plastic, and don't throw anything away. Apply the Native American buffalo carcass mentality to your own life. Not willing to do that? It's the corporations and private individuals who need to change, not you? I thought we didn't have an American aristocracy. I thought we rejected the idea of a monarchy. Sit down and let real people live.

See what they both do, dear reader? They give us a tangible, but not entirely immediate threat. Said vaguely tangible threat justifies them being in control, having the resources at their disposal to fight said threat, said threat doesn't happen while they are in power, so their efforts must have worked, right? Meanwhile, untold millions of Americans in all sizes, shapes, and colors continue to suffer with immediate and crushing needs. Stopping something that is happening already is a lot harder for them than stopping something that isn't happening regularly, if at all.

Should we combat terrorism? Absolutely. When it happens here we should bring the perpetrators to justice, or kill them if that's not possible. We should be vigilant on the home front and take appropriate measures in accordance with what a free and ordered citizenry is willing to put up with. Should we have ships, troops, bases, planes, drones, and secret operatives holding a gun to the metaphorical head of the nations of the world who don't have their stuff together? Absolutely not. It doesn't fix their problems for them and probably has something to do with the fact that when they have some resources they spend them plotting against us. Look to your own house, leaders, before you look to the house of your neighbor. If it is in disarray, leave your neighbor be.

Should we be good stewards of this world? Absolutely. I'm a Christian and I believe this world was given to us to order and oversee, not to destroy. Destruction is in the power of the creator, and we are not that. This is one of the reasons I don't identify as a republican. I don't believe we have free reign to irresponsibly tear down and destroy in the name of money. If that means we stop manufacturing products for a while because we have too many already, so be it. I'd love to put a moratorium on building new houses and commercial buildings in this country until all the unoccupied ones are either renovated and occupied (maybe even with homeless people, (be still my heart!)) or torn down and recycled. The government subsidizes farming so much that they often pay farmers not to grow crops. They can do the same to developers on a temporary basis. Revolutionary ideas, remember? When I think about all the things I could be happy living without but which I have spent time and money acquiring, I am ashamed. It's why I don't shop on Black Friday. I won't greatly inconvenience myself and abide shirking and jostling in an obnoxious crowd to get a deal on some cheaply made product I don't need. We have so much junk lying about being unused that at some point we really should take a hard look at slowing down our manufacturing and consumption. At the very least, it would give those who still categorize Chinese (while we're on the topic of people who are not good stewards of their land...) and Mexican jobs as "stolen" something to feel good about for a bit.

Consumerism is not anti-conservatism. Honest and hardworking men should engage in trade with each other. We are beyond consumerism though. Consumptionism is anti-conservatism, by very definition and the words involved. How can you conserve when you do nothing but devour? That question isn't rhetorical. I want you to compose your answer in a well-worded essay and mail it to me. Route it through my temporary office at the North Pole. I go there sometimes to sit and brood in my Fortress of Peace and Quiet. It's right next to Superman's possibly more famous fortress. Sometimes we declare fake war on each other and have a few hours' fun lobbing snowballs at each other. I usually win but I know he's letting me win. He's quite the guy. Back on track we go.

I believe that the fear of the Lord is the beginning of wisdom. There are very few things on this earth I think about regularly in a fearful state of mind. I don't fear terrorism. I live in Flint, Michigan. It's not a strategic target for terrorists. Those places that are still have multitudes of people living in them, so they clearly don't fear terrorism enough to move and disperse. I applied a smidge of logic there, a practice I want memorialized on my tombstone. Maybe if we all spread out enough, the terrorists will get confused, and do the Charlie Brown head-drooping sad walk home.

I don't fear climate change. I live in Flint, Michigan. Short of some cold winters, we don't have a problem with nature trying to kill us. I don't have to worry about earthquakes, tornadoes, hurricanes, and alligators in my bathtub. Call me biased, but frankly I don't understand why people don't permanently settle here from other places, even in the Midwest. Michigan's lake effect makes it so the cold weather and snow doesn't last for weeks at a time in the winter, and our summers are temperate and pleasant. Maybe if everyone moved to Michigan (our upper peninsula is like a second, secret, really white (but not hateful white) country where people peek out from behind the pine trees to enjoy a hearty Cornish meat pie)(is it distracting to put parenthetical phrases inside parenthetical phrases?) mother nature would get confused and focus her efforts on fixing the Arctic. Terrorism and climate change are the new forms of duck and cover. A threat tangible enough to hand over power and sometimes freedom, but far enough away to not really impact day-to-day life. I have to be diligent about people messing with my possessions, shooting me in the face, beating my kids up at school, or running a red light and T-boning me (Michigan drivers are rascally). I don't think about terrorism and climate change nearly as much as those things. But D's and R's don't have any solutions for those and other everyday problems. It's one of several reasons they are not to be trusted. Once they start working on them, we can start rationing out our trust again.

This book is a rejection of dogmatic and entrenched support of either party. On top of the reasons I list above, their constant, disingenuous clawing for the moral high ground is rendered moot by the corruption, scandals, and outlandish chicanery, and comes across as nothing more than a thinly veiled attempt to get just one more day's intoxicating fix of power. The American people must move beyond looking to the great ones to solve our problems. They have failed us for so very long.

Money

Taxes

Since we have glanced upon the subject of accepted science, can we all agree that the tax code is needlessly complex, and that we are overtaxed? Can at least 97% of us agree without getting the scientists or 9 out of 10 dentists involved? Cool beans.

Our forefathers threw the Boston Tea Party due to taxation without representation. They set in motion a chain of events that founded the most prosperous powerful nation to ever exist that didn't also attempt to conquer the known world. Yes, my Native American ancestors and my African-American brothers' and sisters' ancestors were tragic victims in that whole process, but the premise still stands. America didn't branch out in all directions like the empires of the ancient, middle, and modern worlds to rape, pillage, plunder, and subjugate all others far and near. They used the land and resources at their disposal and accomplished this with hard work and trade. Mistakes were made, yes. No one's denying that. Chill out, keyboard warriors. Where was I? Oh yes, representation. Bostonians also were upset about a 3% increase in tax. That's a good amount, but compared to what we pay now would be a luxury. By the time some people are done paying various taxes, half of their income goes to the gumment. That's a travesty. Honest, dependable, innovative, industrious, responsible people should be able to keep as much of their hard-earned money as possible to dispose of as they wish. I'm not a republican so I think that a certain level of wealth is tacky, and that worshipping money is immoral. A commonly misquoted biblical passage actually states that the love of money, not money itself, is the root of all evil. God allows for the earning and saving of wealth. He even gives specific rules to believers for the usage of said wealth. He doesn't say that it's evil. He says that replacing worship of Him with worship of money is evil.

Liberals have their own issues with wealth. Many of them are fabulously wealthy, but much of their constituency sees the wealth of corporations and individuals in a negative light. Notice that they don't get all huffy about flashy sports stars and entertainers, though. Maybe because some of them worship celebrities, and maybe because the rest understand that the majority of celebrities swipe right for the DNC. A common problem with the progressive wealth-redistribution crowd is that they call amassing wealth evil and immoral. But they have no standard. They can't agree on how much wealth is too much, and were they too, the number would constantly change anyway due to inflation. I have said and will continue to say that I'm no republican. However, the logical problem with many democrats is they call heaps of wealth obscene or immoral. One of the necessary items for a moral stance is a clear definition. Golly, but logic needs to be required school curriculum. There is not a set, agreed upon amount of wealth that is immoral. Next time someone says "immoral wealth", ask them to define a dollar/possession amount at which it becomes immoral. And don't accept "I know it when I see it" as an answer. Pin them down to define an amount and challenge them to pistols at dawn if they can't. Moral stances and judgments require a concrete standard. Many people who used this verbiage when discussing wealth haven't defined this standard. They just know that the rich should pay for their college tuition. I agree, but in a roundabout way. Slow down, conservatives. I'll explain later, if you can let the blood stop accumulating in your face long enough to hear me out.

I'm also not a democrat so I think that the wealth of the rich, if not ill-gained, should remain at the disposal of the rich. By the time that people are done clamoring for the money belonging to the rich, they could have gone out and earned their own. I can't take my money with me to heaven, but I also should be free to make it without restriction so long as I don't rob, harm, or break the law to acquire it. I don't want redistribution of the wealthy's resources because as someone who works full time and runs his own business, we might come through so many levels of redistribution that I'd be one of the rich ones and it'd be my turn to have my stuff seized by noodle-armed men with hair buns.

So anyway, taxes. I see it as the government's role in this discussion to ensure that I can make as much as I want freely, take as little as possible, and still provide for my safety and security, bring justice to those who harm me, then enact and enforce reasonable laws that keep up with technology, industry, and don't infringe on the free and lawful acquisition of that sweet cheddar. Our government has not only grown to the point that it over-taxes and overspends but it's also terribly inefficient. Don't agree? It's become a common thing to rate smartphone apps, take customer surveys, and give feedback on business interactions. Tell me a government service that you would give five stars to. Don't worry, I'll wait. One exception is the Post Office. I like the Post Office and would consider them a speedy, efficient service. Let's look at that one logically. I'm not Greek but I have a modicum of logic. What does the Post Office that other government agencies don't? Private sector competition in the form of FedEx, UPS, and others. I'll let you do the math on that one.

So, taxes. Smarter people than I have postulated that a flat, and not a sliding scale for taxes would be beneficial as it would yield the greatest results. I don't know if this is true, but we tried the sliding scale and it's only gotten more complex and oppressive. In addition, we tried the sliding income tax, all while the constitution never gave the federal government power to tax personal income. So there's that. Lucy's got some 'splainin to do. But anyway, said smart people have put forth a number even. They say 19% flat tax is the sweet spot for returns, and not overtaxing to get in the way of commerce. Let's go with that. The number is not as important as encouraging people to work hard and enrich the lives of others.

Deductions

I'M A BUSINESS owner and my supplies used for business are deductions. When I give to my church or a charity that's deducted. When I buy supplies for my job it's tax deductible. Two of those things are business related. One of them is not. Charity is generosity and helpfulness toward the needy or suffering. When I can add to my financial standing by making donations to charity, my motivations for doing the deed are skewed, thereby making it uncharitable. Generosity is not generosity if done with the promise of a return. That's a business transaction. Government could save itself and the American taxpayer money by removing the deduction for charitable transactions. Donations to churches and the like would then truly be altruistic, as they could only be made in a spirit of charity at that point, not the promise of a return. Sure, this would dramatically lower the amount of money given to charities. But what is left would be charity untainted by ulterior motives, and humans (even those who exist on charity) have a wonderful ability to adapt to changes in situation. This is probably an unpopular idea, but I'm filing this under the "every little bit counts" concept. Maybe even the promise of extra votes attached to your name, increasing commensurately with the amount of your charitable donations, would be a good enough incentive to ensure their widespread continuation.

Some folks out there cannot abide the idea of giving charitably without the government giving an incentive. I just think we could help our government dig itself (themselves? I'm not sure of the proper pronoun here) out of the gargantuan hole it/they have dug for itself/themselves by ending the idea that we can get the money back we give charitably. I'd be more than willing to give folks who give away their money to causes another vote based on the percentage they've given. A person who makes $100,00 per year who gives $10,000 to an altruistic cause has given more than the millionaire who also gives $10,000. This is the lesson to glean from the story of the widow's mite in Mark chapter 12 (LOOK IT UP!). They shouldn't be given the same size incentive, and the government doesn't have to shoulder the burden at tax time of paying these persons back. This might even encourage the "immorally rich" billionaires my Facebook feed won't stop screeching about to start solving problems with their mountains of cash instead of hoarding it and giving the 21st century version of the Bolsheviks (a long enough time since the fall of the horrific Russian Communist machine having elapsed for them to have forgotten or never even learned the lessons of Communism) a reason to drum up class warfare. If they really are the "1%", the extra votes we give to them really won't make a lick of difference in elections. And neither of the major political parties has the ultra-rich vote sewn up anyway. Tax revenues increase, people still can get something in return for their "charity", and some charitable organizations can survive this drastic change while still helping the poor and downtrodden. Like the hilarious "Conflict Resolution" episode of *The Office*, I'd call this a win-win-win.

Will this possibly lead to some charities being shut down? Why, yes it would, asker of rhetorical questions that resides in a dark corner of my mind. Oh well. Have you looked at a financial chart of prominent charities, specifically the leadership salaries and actual amount of each dollar that is used for the need they are addressing? It's horrific in some cases. On top of that, they aren't doing much good with nonstop handouts. Handouts are consumable items. Being taught the skills how to solve one's problems is not. It's a way to generate more consumable items on your own without leaning on your fellow man to provide. I'd like to see more charities which do this. They are out there but are the exception. It's like the old saying goes, give a man a fish and he'll eat for a day. Teach a man to fish and he'll probably be healthier but ultimately less happy due to the reduction in mouth-watering red meat from his diet.

I'm a Christian, but I would see churches and other religious organizations lose their tax exempt status. One reason is that is already probably coming. Along with that inevitability is going to be the idea that if you're only allowed to exist at the state's behest, you'll only be allowed to preach and teach what the state allows you to. China; that too-far-ahead-of-the-pack country to even be seen by the rest in terms of human rights violations, already does this. They will permit your religious organization to function so long as you submit your sermon outlines and keep from criticizing the state and its secular dogma. The churches who don't do this aren't given protection and can be shut down at a moment's notice, along with their leaders conveniently disappeared. Think you have stress in your life worthy of a daily dose of Xanax? Try living peacefully in a country run by a communist regime, and being in violation of that regime's firmly, some might say scarily, held beliefs. The problem with state dogma pushing up against religious doctrine is that at some point a church/synagogue/mosque, preaching in consistency with their guiding document, is going to say some things from their moral system that are uncomfortable to hear. Being a man who struggles physically, emotionally, and psychologically daily with weight and food, I squirm in my seat (as I should) when a preacher talks about proper nutrition, diet, exercise, and management of the body. Fortunately I'm Baptist and don't have to hear sermons on food all that often.

If for no other reason than limiting the time you spend reading this book, let's stop making jokes and get right down to the real argument. People in society and government who are homosexual are uncomfortable with religious organizations preaching that the physical expression of their sexuality is sin. Had to be said. The problem is that they are acting in a way which would suggest that preaching in consistency with a faith's sacred text is unacceptable to them and is the same as discriminatorily removal of freedoms of LGBTQ persons, possibly even persecution. I disagree, especially because people of faith aren't committing acts of violence against others when they preach what they believe to be the truth, and a person wishing to be married in church but not allowed because of the nature of their relationship has a multitude of options beside the one church in that vicinity/sector/quadrant/field of view that is citing their conscientious objection to performing that ceremony. When a person cites their religious views as justification for violence or a church incites violence against others, we already have laws on the books to punish that person or persons in the justice system. Saying that the simple preaching of your faith is contrary to mainstream or governmental norms is policing speech and thought. That's a bird which won't fly. I'd suggest churches give up their tax exempt status with the condition that freedom of their religious preaching and practicing be legally guaranteed at the same time. Churches someday will have an overreaching government remove their tax exempt status anyway, and at that point the idea of having religious and speech freedoms preserved will be a moot point. They will have already been destroyed. Power to tax implies power to destroy. Our republic is strong enough for this area of the law to be adjusted to benefit all without harming one or the other.

Citing the "prohibiting the free exercise" clause from the first amendment to enjoy tax exempt status is whistling after a dog that just won't hunt, in my humble, folksy-saying-inspired opinion. Taxation on personal income; not even a right of the government explicit in the Constitution, doesn't prohibit or discourage people from earning money. But the bigger and harder to solve problem here is one of perception. Non-believers tend to lump religious lunatics and lawbreakers in with the untold millions of Christians who attend church, work hard, love and help their fellow man, and faithfully bring to life the fruits of the Spirit. I believe this is due to comprehensive and targeted (yet not altogether undeserved) media coverage when abuse occurs. The perception is affected when combined with many individuals' already extant search for a reason to discredit religious affiliation wholly. It's not fair, but it's reality.

The systemic abuses of the Catholic Church, terrorist acts masterminded in mosques and neo-nazi groups, and religious hate groups like the kooks at Westboro Baptist have not gone unnoticed or unpunished by the media and justice system. I'd say that giving up tax-exempt status would be a good faith gesture on the part of true Christians and other religions practiced here which don't enjoy the same number of adherents or societal influence as Christianity. Sort of like telling the country they are on the up-and-up and have no conversation with systems like those just mentioned. Also, it would give a reason for non-believers, atheists, agnostics, and secularists to reconcile in their hearts the existence and importance of religion and the concomitant influence it brings to the societal and government tables, *sans* the appearance of special or preferential treatment.

I dream one day of starting and overseeing a private Christian school with free tuition in the inner cities which serves underprivileged youth who only have less than desirable public schools to choose from. This is because private schooling, whether religious or secular, is the province of the upper middle class and the wealthy. I believe with a safer environment to learn and achieve, many students who would otherwise be caught in the cycle of poverty and the horrors of slum living would have a chance to blossom and excel. I want that school to be left alone by the government, outside of accreditation accountability. Removing the tax exempt status of that organization is one way to keep that dam from popping holes and eventually bursting. Weird and impractical dream, you say? I've got goofier ones. I dream one day of standing on a performance stage, and addressing a crowd of gatherers not by their individual names, nay, but by the city where the concert venue is located. "Helloooooo Detroit, Michigan! Y'all having a good time?!" (even though most of our venues are in the suburbs of Detroit and not in the actual city). Failing that, I'd settle for going on a late night talk show and spouting off city names just to hear the audience cheer at the mention of one they are from, have been to, heard about, or just want to cheer because the person next to them is. Had enough or do you want to hear more? Disavowed by the country he was sworn to protect, living a life on the lam, chased by the very men who trained him, Waldo has grown weary of running and is hidden somewhere in this poorly written and sure to be a future prop for uneven sofas. Find him and he'll reward your efforts with my personal email address. Shoot me an electronic communiqué and I'll fill you in on the other goofy dreams I have.

Government *should* be in the business of encouraging proper citizenship. I can't count how many times I've had to answer students who are messing up one of the two major categories to their studies. I worked in a school where many students are apathetic to academic achievement. They come to class, put their heads down, sit with a blank stare on their faces, refrain from raising their hands, keep under the radar, and they don't make waves. These are the kids whose names I forget years after they've left my class. When confronted about their failing grades, they counter with "But I don't act up like some of these other kids".

Now, there are students who come to class and act a mess. They interrupt, goof around, talk, play on their phones, sass mouth their teachers, disrespect their peers, and generally show that they lack in home training and the built-in respect society asks of people heading out into the public every day. But they do get their work done. They are often brilliant kids to whom academics come easily, and problem-solving skills come so quickly that they get bored and seek out attention in negative ways. When confronted about their atrocious behavior, they counter with "But I get my work done".

Both of these students are lacking in one of the two main categories I hinted at above; academics and citizenship. Academics asks you to pick up, practice, and maintain the problem-solving skills we teachers are offering and which adulthood so often requires. Citizenship asks you to be a respectful, civilized member of society, and engage in dignified human interaction without treading over, harming, or picking the pocket of your fellow man. The former is tied to pragmatism, the latter to morality. Both of them are essential to professional, personal, interpersonal, emotional, and spiritual success once students are out of my care and protection.

Government assumes that by the time a person is graduated from high school, they have acquired maturity in both academics and citizenship. However, they reward sloth in academics (see the chapter on welfare) and only punish poor citizenship. Government needs to reward proper citizenship. This is where incentives in the form of deductions could come in. It's obvious to anyone reading to this point that I am a man of strong moral stances, stemming from my Christian faith. We Americans can argue morality until the cows have come home, taken their evening meal, bedded for the night, been milked in the morning, born their young, been slaughtered and turned into delectable steaks, and we still might not come to consensus. We often do argue morality. See any comment stream on a Facebook post as evidence of this statement. Christians would argue that our bodies are not our own and therefore subject to proper stewardship (though many of us fail miserably on that front). Secularists would argue that our bodies are our own and subject to only our own desires (though many do take care of their bodies, having adopted the idea we are only comprised of matter and we should see to its care). However, we can quickly come to agreement on what is responsible. Government should take this concept and run with it, encouraging people to be responsible citizens, both in personal interactions and use of their own bodies.

Another option in lieu of deductions off of taxes for the model citizens among us is giving them more political power. In a republic that is democratically operated, the simplest way to do that is to give the most responsible citizens who take care of their health, avoid trouble, give to charity, and help their fellow man more than one vote. Why not? The Democratic party does this in their primaries with super delegates, whose votes account for more than normal delegates. I imagine the super delegates banding together and fighting the Super Friends in the daydream moments of my day when I should be concentrating on the task at hand. One might argue that we want the most moral and responsible among us to have more of a say, but we don't even need to bring that up (forgive me for doing so). Actually, I'm going to continue in that line of thought for one more sentence. Not including that sentence I just wrote, and this sentence fragment. It seems to me that more and more, the most immoral and irresponsible amongst us are given a say and are looking for ways to dominate those who live healthy, clean, quiet, responsible lives.

I want people to have a really juicy incentive for being the best possible version of themselves. Having your one vote count as more than one is a fabulous way to do that. And there should be a gradual upward scale for a citizen who continues year after year to maintain a clean record and avoid self-inflicted health problems. China is beginning to impose state mandated measures which continue to take away the population's freedom of self-governance. This is not that. This is the government dangling a carrot to encourage the most responsible form of self-government.

Here are some of the areas government should encourage responsible citizenship with personal incentives.

We have a huge problem with obesity in America. Heart disease and obesity related ailments are the pilot fish to the shark of luxurious, affluent civilization. Government should provide a tax deduction for those who can prove with regular checkups that they take care of their bodies and maintain healthy eating, exercise, and activity habits. It is they who are in good shape and energetic that are the most productive at their work, take the fewest days off for sickness, and help their fellow man the most in their free time. There is a popular song out now that reads "Slow songs are for skinny women of loose sexual scruples, I'm a thick female dog, I need tempo". That's all well and good, but what happens when as a large person you get winded dancing to a song before the bridge even hits? It's bound to be embarrassing. Having swallowed the lie of Freud and his disciples that self-esteem is paramount to the cultivation and continuation of one's emotional health, our culture has gone a bridge too far. Not content with shouting "fat shaming" at any mention of weight and proper weight management, rotund people among us can be heard skinny shaming slender people. I just don't get this. I'm a very happy and confident person and have been overweight more of my adult life and teenage years than not. I dislike my flab and was bullied about it as a teenager but I don't and haven't ever gotten depressed or suicidal over it, even in my emotionally weaker younger years. I realize I'm not everyone and can't project my coping skills on everyone because many folks actually have chemical and physiological imbalances in their brains which seriously impede coping skills, but they are the exception.

I believe in moral and responsible management of the body. Now, we cannot come to consensus on moral management but we shouldn't need nine out of ten dentists or 97% of climate scientists to agree before we understand that our obesity is irresponsible. Where our country's productivity and overall quality of life is concerned, it is neither a common, nor an individual good. I do not here propose punitive measures for being obese. A strong government that protects freedoms can encourage people to improve themselves without stepping on their self-governance. Rather, I propose governmental incentives for being healthy. Not from a standpoint of condescension but one of self-admonishment and a desire to "do better", to use a parlance of the times. Lord save us from ourselves if this short section makes me the most virulent enemies.

Telling people at a young age that they should

seek to always be improving themselves will get our nation's youth away from the poorly veiled self-worship our celebrities; America's version of the old-world aristocracy, are teaching them. It will also teach some folks along the way to not model their lives after such folk; something our culture sorely needs. Body positivity is good in the short term so one doesn't get down on oneself, but saying "I'm perfect" denotes the lack of a need to change. I have many friends in their seventies and eighties. Don't judge me. Old people rock, albeit slower and more deliberate in the rocking. Both of my grandfathers died before I was born and both grandmothers were gone by age eight. I have always been eager to make older friends as a result. The wisest friends in their twilight years say "I don't intend to stop improving until the Lord takes me". The least wise "I'm old and stuck in my ways". A generation that is told to constantly change, strive, fail, pick themselves up, and try again to reach their better selves will certainly have more excellent mental health than the self-esteem first crowd.

We have a huge problem with substance abuse in America. Drunken driving, drug abuse, addiction, prescription pill abuse, and smoking all lead to untold thousands of deaths every year. Not to mention the domestic, emotional, professional, and economic suffering for those who don't die, along with their families. Government should provide a tax deduction for those who lead a quiet life of sobriety and can prove with regular testing that they don't put poisons into their bodies. It is they who don't ingest poisons who have the disposable income to start businesses, invest in the market, donate to charities, are given the most lucrative and inexpensive life insurance policies, help their children in the early adulthood years, live longer, fuller, and happier lives, and die without draining the health industry of resources.

We are a nation of self-governance. That means we have a vast array of freedoms not available to those living under more intrusive or less protective governments. But you have to take the good with the bad. Without autocratic oversight, we Americans tend to be more irresponsible with our bodies; the only possession which stays with us all our lives. I'm not saying that government should force us to be better. That would violate our inalienable rights. Government should incentivize responsible use of our bodies. I talk more about this later in the book also. Our leaders have been subsidizing irresponsible choices for so long people have come to rely on government, doctors, and the charity of others to cover for their choices. An old adage of politics states that you get more of what you encourage and subsidize. Without violating individual freedoms, government can certainly find a way to get more responsible behavior from Americans.

We have a huge problem with an aging citizenry that isn't replacing workers. The socially and economically elite typically don't have many children. The middle class (a natural pipeline for breeding young people to enter the workforce) is diminishing. The poor among us are not sending as many of their children into promising careers capitalism would prefer. Abortion has robbed the country of 60 million citizens. People are living longer and longer but not retaining the strength to handle strenuous working activity into old age. South Americans, while being family-centric and in large part Catholic (a church that discourages abortion and birth control), are having more babies than any other demographic in the Americas, but we aren't letting them into the U.S. (more, much more, on this later) in numbers to replace a declining population.

What do we do? Social Security is doing some of the heavy lifting, but there's no promise of that being around forever. It also doesn't fully financially support a person who wishes to retire in comfort. Said person having to rely on savings, pensions, retirement funds, charity, and the help of churches and family to fill in the gaps.

The first long-term solution with effects many years down the road is hitting young people hard with ways to save, scrimp, and be more fiscally sound through our education system. I've got a spreadsheet formula on my home computer I use which adjudicates 35% of every paycheck to savings, retirement, and stock options, 40% to *paying ahead* on my bills (a novel concept, unfortunately) and debts, and allocating the leftover 25% to gas, groceries, incidental expenses, and any remainder to leisure, fun, and entertainment. Half a year of practicing this budgeting with only my meager landscaping income from June to November 2018 and I had paid my bills through January 2019 by November, with a little savings leftover. Now that I'm finishing this book in the first part of 2019, I think of what I can do with this kind of fiscal responsibility for the rest of my life. Working hard and saving really isn't all that difficult in this country. It just seems so to those who want government to do everything for them.

The second, and more immediate solution to this problem is to incentivize people to take care of the elderly and infirm. It's a harsh reality that some people will escape to old age without any significant savings. The wide margin in quality between retirement home options is stark evidence of that. I should like to posit that family is the immediate place to look for this, NOT THE GOVERNMENT. Excuse the yelling. You'll see several times in this book, if you have the patience, fortitude, wherewithal, and ample headache medication to finish it, that I put very little faith in the government as it currently exists to solve people's problems. That's where the family comes in. Family is the closest, first, strongest, and last line of defense against calamity and loss of ability/possession/livelihood. Though parents retiring to live in the homes of their grown children is fodder for many a dramedy movie, I'd say it's the best way to handle what can only be described as foolish and misguided continued reliance on government to solve the problem. I get really attractive tax credits for being the head of my household, the only meaningful earner, and the supporter of minor children who aren't expected to support themselves. The same should be true for family and friends who do the same for the aging parents of this country. Those who have deceased, disabled, incarcerated, or indigent children and no family friends should be able to apply for government relief facilitated by the donations and efforts of companies, corporations, and people of means who would like, at the very least, to take advantage of this incentive, if not do something altogether altruistic. Future generations need not fret for their golden years and whether or not Uncle Sam will be there to fetch them their cane and slippers.

We have a huge problem with civil unrest, rejection of authority, and irresponsible driving in America. Protesters have forgotten the meaning of peaceful assembly. Police are maligned, derided, scorned, assaulted, and sometimes even killed for holding the thin line between order and chaos. Our urban schools are a pipeline to prisons. Texting, speeding, and aggressive driving lead to all sorts of suffering. Allstate insurance gives its clients a safe driving bonus; basically cash for not being dumb behind the wheel and incurring their service extra costs. It is they who only assemble peacefully (if they must assemble), accept the authority of police (yes, this is a touchy subject and I will address it later), refrain from criminal activity, and never get in accidents or acquire speeding tickets who keep the system from slowing down and using up valuable resources. Government should provide a tax reduction for those who keep their nose clean and don't make foolish mistakes. This deduction could grow each consecutive year of responsible citizenship, along with keeping one's children out of legal trouble.

For the love of crumb cake, government could even give an escape clause to those who get the occasional traffic violation or serve their prison sentences and change their lives for the better. I have gotten four tickets in the last two years. Before these occurrences, I've gotten out of half a dozen or more. I'm not proud of this, on the contrary, rather ashamed. However, I make a point of being respectful to all policemen. Not just out of a pragmatic desire for self-preservation and refusal to needlessly provoke someone who carries a gun and has extreme stress every day at work, but also out of basic human respect. I recognize that officer as a fellow image-bearer of God, and therefore deserving of dignity and respect without having to earn it with me. I find the idea of having to "earn respect with me" haughty and prideful. God allowed that person an interaction with me, and that person bears God's image. If I put them through rigorous tests in order to earn such a basic thing as respect, I'm placing myself far above them. Furthermore, as a teacher, I'm used to having peaceful and calm interactions stemming from conflict as I serve those who often hate me. All while being horribly underpaid for the service I render to society. I can empathize with cops.

So, the speeding tickets I've not gotten because I obeyed and respected, and engaged the officers in conversation, all while showing regret for my actions. Police look for this. I also commiserate with them. I'm a terribly busy single father of four who has to work multiple jobs to get by. Sometimes I'm running behind and I speed because of it. Not an excuse, but cops are merciful to those who lead difficult lives without resorting to crime. It doesn't hurt that cops and teachers are mistreated by the community they serve, and we can understand each other better due to this.

Now, the tickets I have gotten I fully deserved. My disappointment at being pulled over doesn't overmaster my reason and respect. I received one in Pontiac for expired tags, one for speeding while driving my Uber customers in the neighborhoods of Rochester and Warren, Michigan, and one for going way over the limit on the highway in Ohio. I was at fault all three times and deserved the consequences for my choices. In all of these instances, I've made sure to swallow my pride, shake the hands of officers, and thank them for doing their jobs.

For the Ohio one, I had my kids in the car. Our children are always watching and absorbing what we do. I can't preach respect for authority in my home and not practice said respect when I take them out into the world. Government could give an incentive for those of us who speed and get caught by saying that if you do get pulled over, positive and respectful interaction with the police can still qualify you for this deduction. We are in an age of personal recording devices in the possession of police and the citizenry, so reviewing and judging these interactions can be handled quite easily.

We have a huge problem with the plight of criminals. Many of them return to crime once they are released because no one wants to help them out. Our prison system isn't doing it, nor are business owners and people of means who refuse to accept former convicts as employees, nor are former convicts themselves who have a tremendous rate of recidivism once they are released. Government does a little bit to entice people of means with tax incentives to employ former criminals...and...that's about it. I address prisons a little later. When it comes to personal choices on the part of reformed convicts, they should receive the same incentive as the citizens who never commit crimes. If they can stay clean and proper, disassociate themselves from personal connections to crime, acquire and maintain gainful employment for years and years, why should their record stay with them? We should have a system of expungement once a person has paid their debt to, and shown they can be a productive, moral part of society. I shall recount a personal story which exemplifies this.

In the early summer of 2017, I was struggling to keep up with my work. I taught until 4pm in Pontiac, drove home almost an hour to Flint, then worked like a madman to cut my customers' lawns, trees, hedges, and finish other jobs by the time the sun went down. I was spending all of my Saturdays and Sundays catching up on work. My employees were unreliable, had other jobs, or no transportation. Customer projects were stacking up and constantly being pushed back. I realized I needed a partner and not employees. One of the reasons I believe in God is that He has made Himself known to me in very real ways on many occasions. This was one such an occasion.

On the north side of Flint, I had a customer who wanted two trees on two different properties cut down. Both trees were right next to a house and required finesse. On the south side of Flint, I had a customer with the same kind of job. Not owning a boom lift, I rented one from a local business and scheduled all three jobs on the same day, intending to cut down on rental costs and maximizing profits. Using it to prune the limbs of the south side customer, I told them I would be back and headed to the north side. Upon arrival at their house, the hydraulics on the boom malfunctioned and I realized I'd have to return it and schedule the job for another day, as the daylight was waning. Turning the corner too sharply in sight of the customer's house, the boom went up on the curb and was turned over. My truck was spared any damage beyond the hitch being bent.

Now, I'm confident in my own skin to never feel uncomfortable wherever I go. I am an outsider in all the places I live and work. I am a middle class single father with a working class mentality, but am part of a very wealthy church with very low rates of divorce. Having four children in tow and working two jobs makes me stand out in such a place. I'm of Native American descent on my mother's side but my features favor my father's Caucasian side. So when I teach, I'm a corny white boy in Pontiac to the African-American and Spanish-American communities. I used to live on the south side of Flint and regularly work in the north side; both are places where I am surrounded by people who don't look like me. I don't look for pity because I've never needed it. My outsider status doesn't matter to me because I have found that no matter their shape, size, or color, all people are looking for respect and love. Having said this, I know that some people are uncomfortable with my upsetting of their day. A white boy on the north side of Flint blocking traffic with a giant piece of equipment could qualify as just this.

As is often the case, many people rolled by without offering help, while several stopped and unsuccessfully tried to help me tip it back up by hand. That is, until Big Johnny B. stopped by and offered his services. He had a truck and tow strap and said he could tip it back up properly. I looked at his truck and saw his company name, logically but mistakenly assuming that he would charge me for his time and effort. I told him that I didn't have any cash on my person but could pay him if given the opportunity to find an ATM. He vehemently refused, stating that he and I were out there just trying to make a buck and he was happy to help. It was but a few minutes later that the lift was righted, hooked up, and I was ready to leave. Johnny ran a service similar to mine and gave me his business card, wishing me Godspeed in my endeavors.

A few days later, I realized that this man should be my partner. I called him and interviewed him, and ascertained that he was looking for a partner also (re: God making Himself known to me). He said that he didn't understand the cutthroat practices and aggressive underbidding that plagues this industry, as there is enough money for all of us. He was up front about his sordid past in the drug dealing game and told me that he could still be in it and making loads of cash but that he was a born again Christian and wanted to make his money honestly and morally. So we partnered that summer and proceeded to rock out with our socks out.

We both have big and strong personalities, have argued and conflicted, but we have always returned to peace when the dust clears. I have gotten him work in the white community he would otherwise be unlikely to acquire customers, and he has gotten me work in the black community I would otherwise be unlikely to acquire customers. We call each other brother and tell each other we love each other. We have both come into the lives of our respective families. We have worked for Spanish, Indian, and Arab customers who I would imagine enjoy seeing racial unity in the name of brotherly love and mutual benefaction. Johnny's criminal past matters not one whit to me, as I should hope my mistakes and transgressions don't matter to those I've offended and hurt. I chose Johnny for a partner when more successful options devoid of criminal pasts were at my disposal (I interviewed about half a dozen guys during this process) but who had greedy attitudes about their customer base and work accounts. I see this as a model for all people looking to move past the mistakes of their youth. Unfortunately, we have a system in which these mistakes stay with you your entire life, and professional, societal, and legal forgiveness are at a premium. When it comes to released and reformed convicts, a period of time (concomitant with the seriousness of their offense(s) lapsed without resorting back to crime should allow their records to be expunged.

Moving on, **we have a huge problem with** divorce and broken families in this country. Conservatives (both black and white) are quick to point out the rate of fatherless homes in the black community, while ignoring the rate of divorce in the white community. Which is worse? I won't venture a guess at answering that question because pointing fingers isn't all that productive when one has personal faults to address. I will say that both lead to the breakdown, denigration, and the loss of sacredness for the family. I find it ironic that when I was forced into divorce and a bitter custody battle, I was taken to "family court". What a horrific misnomer. A legal setting that allows the expedient and relatively easy breaking up of families (Michigan is a no-fault divorce state) should not be called family court, but I digress. Government should create deductions for those families who decide to work out problems and conflicts and remain intact for the sake of everyone involved (not just the kids). Or, in the case of families started without marriage, government should create deductions for those parents who are productive and survive without taking welfare assistance, thereby not draining the system and taxpayers of resources. It's a proven statistical fact that stable families breed stable people, which in turn breed more stable families. Despite the moral objections of many religious people, marriage rights have been extended to all people. Government should incentivize those who get married, stay married, and work with their spouses through all the trials and tribulations that are sure to arise (for better *or worse*, remember?), or those who take on the burden of raising children alone and band together with their children to accomplish the same goal without needing government to step in and perpetually lend a helping hand.

We have a huge problem with small businesses

in this country. Many fail due to overarching govern-ment regulations and taxes. I am of the mind that someone who steps out of their comfort zone, takes a huge risk, and attempts to gainfully provide products and services to others without great resources backing them, shouldn't have to pay income taxes, especially when the money to start and operate this business often comes from working a day job for someone else during the developmental years of the business. Government should remove all income tax for small businesses which make under a certain amount of money. They should also ease up on restrictions and regulations, something which the current administra-tion is actively engaged in.

Steven Crowder, a popular conservative podcast-er, is fond of pointing out that higher minimum wages and increased government regulations are liberal and progressive in nature, legislated by the same people who pontificate about the "evil" corporations that are destroying the middle class. However, these same corporations support liberal and progressive legisla-tion (Don't believe me? Spend some time researching liberal corporate political activism) because they are the only businesses who can afford to pay higher min-imum wages and adapt to tighter (re: more expensive) regulations. So the great ironic tragedy here is that the same people who decry the fate of small businesses have a direct hand in their downfall ideologically, practically, or legislatively. Goodness gracious, how I wish logic was a more common skill.

We have a huge problem with increasing sloth in this country. Laziness is already our default setting as humans. We have to force ourselves to work hard. Increasingly, mediocrity and just doing the bare minimum are accepted as, well, acceptable, especially in the name of "sticking it to the man". I believe this, very subtly, is contributing to the decline of the middle class, as the hardworking and well-off further distance themselves from the lazy and indigent. Each generation is becoming less skilled with their hands and more entitled to leisure time. Don't believe me? Look at what cell phones are doing to the collective work ethic of our culture. I'm guilty in this respect myself, so I'm not preaching from a standpoint of condescension but one of shared guilt. Government should create a way for each citizen to have a federal resume, so to speak, so that employers can report a person's work habits to the appropriate agency and reward a person for being the best possible version of themselves while on the clock, thereby earning rewards in the deduction game.

Same goes for people who leave jobs in responsible fashion. Someone who finds a better job and gives their employer a proper notice should not feel as if they are wronging anyone by bettering their life station. As a sort of checks and balances measure, workers should be able to report companies with irresponsible hiring, firing, and layoff practices, giving them a federal resume also. I remember the last office job I had. I was going through a divorce and horribly depressed due to the factors involved. My employer, when they laid me off, gave me a month's salary, despite laying me off on the 8th day of the month. Companies who break ties with employees in the most dignified and gracious manner should be re-warded for recognizing the humanity in the people they engage. Golly gee willikers, we have a license and driving record, a birth certificate, social security number, legal record, and a credit score, why can we not have a work record that keeps track of our positive work habits?

This section is getting lengthy, so I will wrap it up. Morality is a wide and hotly debated subject. Responsibility, not so much. People who refrain from substance abuse, take care of their health, show up on time and work hard every day, and maintain a quiet life of dignity and industry are the ones who enrich society without taking more than their earned share, help their fellow man, send children into adulthood with a leg up on the competition, financially uphold those parts of government we do need, develop and maintain positive, healthy relationships, and retire to enjoy their golden years in peace and self-affirmation, knowing they've run their race with few stumbles along the way. Government should subsidize respon-sible behavior and create incentives for being a model citizen, not just punish citizens who do stumble and fall. Money is a fantastic motivator and we would see an overhaul of irresponsible behavior if our government got its head in the game in this fashion. There should be a "model citizen" deduction which either greatly reduces or eliminates altogether a person's individual tax burden.

Debt

READY TO HAVE your mind blown? Through years of irresponsible (some might argue immoral) spending practices, the federal government finds itself tremendously in debt. Debts only help your credit and credibility when you pay them. Republican and Democratic presidents alike have raised debt ceilings and continued their spending, so much so that drunken sailors would be insulted to be called a president. Now, I don't know much 'bout nothin', but I know that the debt I've incurred in my life isn't necessarily a good thing. It needs to stop, and every little bit counts.

Foreign Aid

Time for another unpopular idea. I'm not an America first person. I'm just a practical person who wishes to live by a moral code greater than myself. New Testament churches since the day of Pentecost have typically elected pastors to teach, admonish, encourage, empathize, and basically take care of the flock. These pastors are generally accepted as leaders. When a pastor's house falls into scandal, recklessness, discord, or immorality, they are often removed from the office. This falls in line with a passage from I Timothy that asks whether a man can take care of the church of God if he cannot manage his own house. Apply that to our government and country in general. We are accepted as world leaders. Bush and Obama were often referred to as the leader of the free world. Countries, civilizations, societies, and businesses adopt the American way of doing things in many of their affairs. Don't believe me? What language is the language of commerce? Exactly.

Here's the problem. Ever increasingly, our own house is in disarray due to scandal, recklessness, discord, and immorality. And, ever increasingly, America is losing its status as a world leader both in theory and practice. We cannot look to the order in the house of another when our own is crumbling. For the fiscal year 2013, we gave $32.53 billion dollars in foreign economic aid (https://en.wikipedia.org/wiki/United_States_foreign_aid). How could the impoverished and crime-ridden cities of Flint, Detroit (sorry, I'm mitten-biased), Chicago, Atlanta, New York, Los Angeles, and countless others use this money? How could the oft-forgotten and casually dismissed rural and impoverished areas of this land use it? How could they *not* use it, given that it is handed over to ethical and responsible people? Could the government begin to pay its debts with that money? Could it just be *saved*? Just because we've done this for so long does it mean we shouldn't stop it? In his opening line to *Common Sense* (the book that sparked a revolution), Thomas Paine stated "a long habit of not thinking a thing *wrong*, gives it a superficial appearance of being *right*, and raises at first a formidable outcry in defence of custom." We have done things the same for so long. It's time for something new.

It's time for us to stop meddling. As I write this section, the movie *Black Panther* is racking up record box office numbers and critical acclaim. It's a marquee moment for minority-driven cinema. The premise of the movie states that if left free of western intervention, African culture could have survived and thrived with unparalleled success. In one of the movie's best humorous moments, Bilbo Baggins is called "Colonizer" by the movie's version of Agent Q. The movie has become a controversial talking point between conservative and liberal commentators, basically making it out to be much more than what it is; a fantastically entertaining movie with some intriguing ideas and speculations. I agree with the premise, historically and contemporarily. We should leave sovereign peoples alone. Just as Europeans colonized and overran Africa, rationalizing their behavior that stemmed from a white savior mentality, so our government meddles in the affairs of the world with an American savior mentality.

In addition, we aren't solving problems with our efforts or money, just getting these nations hooked on it. Much of it is going to unstable countries whose leaders either defraud the people or use it for their own gain. When foodstuffs are freely handed over to unstable countries with questionable laws and a lack of civilized order, the food lands in the hands of warlords and corrupt officials who turn around and use it to further oppress the people. Think the villain in *Mad Max: Fury Road*. He owned the people (and by extension the attractive, fertile women of childbearing age) because he owned the water. This isn't just some Hollywood machination. It happens in real life to the aid we send. When it does land in the hands of the people who need it, it only addresses the problem so long as its benefits last. We are not teaching fledgling nations to be self-sufficient with perpetual aid. The solution to this is we take over the country, force the violent and corrupt out, and run it ourselves, or give the people in these places a lifeline to come here or the option to stay and fend for themselves. The first is just a hop, skip, and a jump from imperialism, no matter our intentions. The second is fair, and in line with the "we are a nation of immigrants" buzz phrase that's been en vogue since Obama popularized it. Do they have to stay in their homelands to preserve their culture and heritage? I know a few Greektowns, Chinatowns, Little Italies, Spanish Harlems, Frankenmeuth's, and other places that would beg to differ.

The point of charity is to remove the need, which

ours hasn't. We give much aid to countries that don't produce (many of them in island locales where fishing and tourism are the major sources of income) but can't (or haven't learned to) sustain their lives without foreign aid. That which does find its way into citizens' hands clearly doesn't change their lives much for the better. Citizens living in these countries could be offered a fast track to American citizenship (using the process I propose in my immigration section) if they want to come to a place where they will have no need of charity and can work and be free to order their lives without constant fear of survival. I contend that our president should be the leader of the USA, not the world. A fearless leader needs to come along and tell the charity cases of the world that they can no longer suck at the American teat. They will probably then have to then start traveling around in the presidential Pope-Mobile in order to dodge the snipers that will come out of the woodwork. People will adapt. They have an uncanny way of doing so. It's sometimes a harsh truth but true nonetheless. I don't advocate not helping the world. I advocate getting things in order here and helping when we aren't in debt. I've never given to charity when I can't pay my own bills. The American government continues to violate this pragmatic principle, placing the bill on the ample but overburdened shoulders of the taxpayer and our grandchildren. Withdrawing aid will help the American taxpayer, and possibly lead to some really upset folks in other places. See below.

Military

ALONG WITH THE economic aid, we gave $10.57 billion the same year in military aid. Does this stabilize the world? I can't say that it does. Things are as they've always been. Much like the worst places in our worst big cities, the violent, aggressive, and opportunistic are still taking advantage of the weak, peaceful, and provincial. We police the world but does it gain us anything? Does it add to our respect, appreciation, and acclaim? Are unstable regions any less so due to our presence? I often tell my students that character is doing what is right when authority isn't watching. My presence restrains kids from fighting, running amok, cursing, and breaking rules. But if they never define, adopt, and practice morality in their own mind, they will only ever not transgress for fear of punishment. This is only surface morality. Same goes for the countries we police. Fear is a motivator but it is tiresome for both parties concerned. We maintain a huge standing army for the sake of immediate and devastating response should violence be enacted against us or an ally. All while many of our own children have no safe place to call home. Unless countries where we maintain a presence can pay for the continuance of protection, we should once again offer any native who doesn't feel safe without us there a fast track to American citizenship and withdraw forces to secure our own borders. We will need it.

Ever since World War II, we have self-applied a mandate to see to the affairs of other sovereign countries. This violates a prophetic warning by George Washington to avoid foreign entanglements. And how has it worked out for us? Communists are still in Vietnam and Korea. The Middle East still has war and instability. Parts of Africa still beholden to warlords, and so on and so forth. We shouldn't be completely isolationist. We should still engage in business. The areas of the world which enjoy peace and stability like large parts of Europe, Asia, and South America are the areas where America engages in trade and which have adopted modern commerce practices. Lord above, the Chinese communists have adapted to include capitalistic practices in order to fund their horribly expensive way of governing. United Arab Emirates enjoys tremendous peace due to their wealth gained from sitting on an ocean of oil. Trade and commerce promote prosperity. This heightens the general welfare, which in turn promotes peace. Who would've thunk it?

Anyway, a violent response to pre-World War II *military* isolationism is certainly possible. Our vast global military could be employed to make sure our land, coastlines, and skies are safe, possibly only necessitating a minor reduction in our military. "Reduction" is a four-letter word to many republicans, but not necessarily a bad thing. After each war leading up to World War II, America always reduced the military. This was done out of necessity, as peacetime doesn't need as large a standing and active army. It was also done to promote peace by not provoking defeated parties into regrouping and retaliating. America didn't sign the Treaty of Versailles because it prophetically saw the breaking up and seizing of German territories by the Allies as motivation for the Deutsch to rise again and settle accounts. After World War II, America retained and grew its military, eventually going on to puff our chests out and engage in schoolyard monitoring. Some would say we became the schoolyard bullies. In many instances, I would say I agree. We are not a conquering empire in the traditional sense, but geopolitical activity has given us the appearance of imperialism. We need to calibrate, bringing to mind the words of Paine. Just because we've been doing it a long time doesn't make it right.

One could make the argument that military isolationism will actually lead to the decline of global terrorism. My republican brothers and sisters are quick to point out that Islam is the epicenter of terrorism and that statistics bear it out and that we need to do this and respond to this and blah blah blah. I say we should leave them alone. Many republicans are either Christian or amenable to Christianity. Many also forget that Christianity commands us to strive towards being at peace with every man. While we are busy trying to bring western ideals to Muslim lands, we forget that maybe they don't care for western ideals, and would possibly get along with us were trade the major reason for interacting. China is rife with oppression and human rights violations but we still engage in trade with them. Remember the long, bloody, and brutal Chinese-American war? Me neither.

Islam is a religion and political ideology. The tenets of Islam, for better or worse, give people a way of governing their personal and family morality, but also governing their state. New Testament Christianity does nothing of the sort. The story of the Old Testament has a through line of the Jewish people time after time rejecting God's governance and wishing for a king of their own as their neighbors had. This led to the eventual decline, conquering, and scattering of Israel. By the time of the New Testament, the Jews were under the control of the Romans. Instead of Jesus Christ coming and overthrowing the Romans (as many of they who looked for the Messiah wished), He gave them a way to overthrow sin in their own lives, govern their churches, manage their families, all while living at peace with the Romans or any other usurpers who may come along. He tells Pontius Pilate that His kingdom was not of this earth, otherwise His followers would have revolted against Roman rule. We American Christians have enjoyed tremendous comfort, peace, and even luxury while many of our laws reflected Christian morality, but that doesn't necessarily make our nation a Christian one. Laws don't save and send sinners to heaven. May we remember that as we gripe about the secularization of our nation.

Islamic states have laws and governance coming straight from their guiding document. While we may disagree with what they do and how they do it, we can still be at peace with them, even engage in trade with them. Paine argued that an honest man doing a day's work accomplished more in a day than any crowned ruffian did in all his years on the throne. This is because honest men who engage in trade with each other don't have to agree on any matter other than bettering the life of someone else in return for proper payment. If our military stops policing the world, maybe the terrorists who hate us and our western ideals will leave us alone. Yes, I know they are responsible for their own choices and atrocities, but flesh excites flesh and they see their crusade as justified partially through our arrogance and meddling.

Goodness sake, Muslims should be some of the staunchest supporters of the Republican Party. Most Muslims are horrified by abortion. Most of them marry (and do not divorce) in their young adult years and believe in the nuclear family that is led by a husband, ministered to by a wife, and puts forth productive and moral children. Many of them distrust the public school system and send their kids to religious private schools. Most of them go to college, ply a trade, or start a business, and engage in capitalistic habits.

Finger-pointing on the part of conservative commentators listing weak reasons why we are incompatible hasn't done anything to endear Christians to Muslims. That's a travesty. Christians should work to be at peace with them because outside of the guiding document and theology, Muslims and Christians agree on the temporal and many of the moral matters of life. Problem is, non-white and non-Christian minorities in this country tend to vote in what they perceive to be in their self interests, and George W. didn't do his party any favors when he started a second war in Iraq. Decent and rational Muslims understood that Osama and his terrorist group did a great evil on 9/11 and supported their being brought to justice. But Bush took it too far, lost focus of the primary objective, started an indescribably costly and ongoing war, and in effect ceded the credit for killing Bin Laden to Hillary and Barack. While not impossible, it'll take a master stroke of bridge-building to move Muslim voting habits to republicans. Based on the common points of morality shared by Muslims and Christians, coupled with Christians' mandate to love all fellow image-bearers of God, it can be done.

Immigration

REFRESH MY MEMORY. Is this a hotly debated issue? I can't remember because I waved to a friend who has been living on Mars under a rock on my way to live under an even larger rock on Pluto while suffering temporary blindness and deafness from sunspot radiation.

I've got a fix that will not make both sides of this debate happy in their currently entrenched positions, but one that will address concerns raised by both sides. Since it is a practical compromise asking both sides to give up something, I'm sure it'll never happen.

It's really frustrating for a politically centrist but morally conservative person like myself to see the Republicans be so dogged and inflexible on this issue. They really should reconsider their rigid stance. Many immigrants move to large cities dominated by democratic voting. Eventually, these cities will have swollen to such sizes and political power that they'll overwhelm Republican strongholds like the Mountain West, plains states, and the South, especially if

Democrats astute enough to recognize their slight numbers advantage get their way and abolish the Electoral College. Republicans should recognize a couple of things about the sheer numbers of illegal immigrants.

First, this is a better argument against totalitarian government than any they could make with their green bean casserole holes. As I write this sentence, there is an ever-growing, ever-more-loudly-screeching wing of the Democratic party that wishes for the government to take more and more power out of the hands of private citizens and place it in that of government. People coming here from corrupt socialist and communist countries aren't coming here to get a better life and then hand control of that life over to the government. They're escaping that. No one frantically builds a raft, shoves off the coast of Florida, lands in Cuba, and praises God they escaped this capitalist nightmare. Immigrants want to come here and order their lives. Right now, the Republican-ts are making sure all the Democrats need to do is promise a few free things and say "we're your friends" in order to lock up their vote.

Second, and to a lesser degree, it's an effective argument against the Catholic Church. Most conservatives are either Protestant or amenable to the Christian cause. I'd say it's understood many of American Catholics are left-leaning. The Catholic Church, having lost its command over Europe, has maintained much of its interests in South America. I make an argument at some other point in this eminently combustible treatise why big government and Catholicism go well together, so I won't repeat myself. I won't repeat myself. To be sure, most immigrants come here and maintain their Catholic faith and practices. But were the Republican Party to fix this thing, they'd secure the immigrant vote for a long while. That'd strike a deadly blow to the despicable "racist white people keep the Republican party alive" argument that's been floating around since the 60's.

There are two ways to emigrate to our great land. One is to go through a huge amount of rigmarole, cost, paperwork, academic learning, and test-taking. The other is to hop a fence, swim a river, hide in a giant ship's storage container, or dig a tunnel, circumventing all of that. It's no wonder more immigrants come here from impoverished countries in Latin America the quick way. No, they aren't coming to a life that is equal to the opportunities conferred on one of full citizenship status, but it certainly has to be better than what they are fleeing (logic, I command thee to return to the collective intellects of the general populace, in the name of the King). That's why they are circumventing the law. This is where conservatives of the Bush and Trump eras (and let's not forget moderates of the Obama and Clinton eras) will bring up the illegal activities they are engaging in once they are here, on top of breaking the law just to come here. I've got a solution to that, if you'll just listen for a minute. Please, please, won't you listen to me? Stop waiting to talk and just LISTEN!

Many do come here and commit crimes. It's no secret that being a criminal often guarantees a fast track to a comfortable life. Most, however, do not. They just want a better life, and low-wage jobs in the USA are even better than no-wage suffering in Latin America. Socialist and Communist governments have done quite a lot to mess up the Latin American world. Try your best not to experience whiplash on this next tangent.

Christianity in the USA is not really all that Catholic. They tried to take over the New World and south of our border is where they largely succeeded. I've got an idea as to why. <u>Any Catholic readers, please, please, do your best to not be offended by the following analysis. I love you and I pray for you. I'm an outsider who has studied your religion very closely and while I cannot ascribe to your faith, I do love you as human beings. I've got Catholic family members and I pray they continue to love and associate with me after reading this.</u> Catholicism is a faith of many precepts, doctrines, practices, and statutes. The two things that can overrule a doctrine or practice are a counsel of the leaders, or the Pope when he is seated in the chair from which he claims to be the conduit of the voice of God. This has happened many times. History of the Catholic Church is rife with retractions, changes, reversals, and sometimes even apologies. This implies a couple things. Firstly, it denotes that

God and His morality changes. This is a major reason why I don't ascribe to Catholicism. I don't believe that God changes what is right and wrong, just and unjust, righteous and unrighteous. It's why as a Christian I can always have a standard to live by, whether or not I fail that standard is another conversation. I always know whether what I'm doing is right or wrong based on an immutable authority above my own. Secondly, it gives the Pope tremendous power over those who follow him. He can tell them whether they should stop doing something, start doing another, stop doing something in one way, and start doing it in another way, and so on. He's a figurehead clothed in tremendous power, determining the day-to-day morality of millions, a morality which, in theory, can change based on something new he decrees.

Now, look at Socialism and its older, more aggressive, albeit vastly more effective brother, Communism. We are creatures of worship, and those who accept governmental rule over every aspect of their lives have convinced themselves that government is the determiner of what is right and wrong. Hence, they worship government. When government retracts or even contradicts itself, it's not a moral dilemma for the follower because government is always right, and can go on changing for the time, the situation, or the need. Orwell's government in *1984* did this constantly, meanwhile demanding blind faith and acceptance by the populace, brainwashing and killing those who fell out of line. Socialist countries often become oligarchies. Communist countries, without exception, become dictatorships. It's no secret being a dictator is a pretty sweet life, akin to an absolute monarch of the old world. Oligarchies can succeed for those in power so long as they have a plan, are like minded in the areas of consequence, and they execute their plan without too much infighting. No matter the paradigm adopted, there is either a small group of powerful people or one ultra-powerful demagogue who determines to the population what they are to do, how to do it, and what to think when they are doing it. Call me reductionist if you want. I'm not writing a treatise on these government forms. I'm trying to solve problems, so let's keep it pushin' baby.

Do you see the parallels between Communism and Catholicism? Both of them require acceptance of a powerful figurehead who runs and orders the lives of their followers. For the Communist dictator, he runs and orders their day-to-day, practical, temporal lives. For the Pope, he runs and orders their spiritual lives. So with every corner of a person's existence fulfilled, it's no wonder Communism and Catholicism can coincide, flourish together, and (arguably) dominate a continent.

It's become a common rhetorical tactic for open-border proponents to say that Christians and Trump supporters (the exact same people in the minds of progressives) should support open immigration because of

Christian love and Jesus and this and that. I agree with them. I'm not a progressive, but I agree. We should support as many people coming from horrible situations who only want to better their life station. An added bonus is that they won't find many Catholic churches here, but will find a multitude of Bible-believing, Bible-preaching churches who will gladly open their doors and show them that obeisance to a Pope and his clergy is not the path to eternal salvation. The evangelical opportunities are limitless. Having said that, I must make allowances to those Christians who don't see the evangelical opportunities as outweighing the risks involved, and those non-Christians who are politically conservative and believe that the rule of law must outweigh Christian matters. A fact which, as a citizen of the USA, I actually will concede to. We Christians are commanded to live within the laws of our land, and follow them unless they command us to do something immoral. So far as I can see, the law of the USA doesn't hold a gun to my head and force me to violate my morality. Once theft, lying, gossip mongering, murder, and others become compulsory, we'll revisit this talk.

Nate, just solve the problem already! I mean, ahem, Nathan Andrew Roberts (you can go by all three names when you're a famous author, serial killer, or new member of SAG and your first and last names also belong to a previous member), *please cease this rhetorical puttering about and describe your solution!*

Here goes.

For the folks who want to emigrate here the legitimate way, we leave the system in place. It's clear when they come here to study, start a business, find a job, marry a spouse, or join a family, that our immigration system works because the overwhelming majority of them inculcate themselves into our country without losing their cultural identity.

For those who want to go the easy route, you make it easy on them but also hold them accountable. As you stop them at the border, government officials process them and ask them what their plan is, where they intend to stay, what they intend to do, with whom they intend to associate, how they intend to live here peaceably and within the laws, give them resources to follow up with, point them in the right direction for learning at least the functional parts of the language (something that should make conservatives happy but for which I don't particularly give a care), and then put them on probation. This isn't a novel idea; it's just never been applied to this part of our culture. New employees, children, students, athletes who make bad choices, and reformed convicts all have to engage in probationary periods. Why not those coming to our country, having yet to prove they intend to contribute, not detract from our great society?

It sounds harsh but outfitting them with ankle monitors, having them report regularly to their governmentally appointed advocates who will also guide them in the process of being a productive citizen, take drug tests, show proof of legitimate income, and monitoring their daily activity is one way to hold them accountable. Doing this for a predetermined amount of time equal to or greater than the work accomplished by the group who take the traditional path to citizenship would give them a chance to prove themselves without having to take the more work-intensive route while allowing them to work, earn wage, cement their lives, marry, raise children, and so on and so forth. Then we really could open our borders in a controlled manner and give the influx of people options for their path to citizenship. This would countermand, weed out, and/or expose those who intend to come here and engage in criminal activities for their provender. It would also provide our government a more compassionate way of interfacing with those who are already here illegally. If they have an incentive to come out of hiding and take a more circuitous route to citizenship, my thought is that most of them would because it would open up opportunities that keeping one's head down, flying under the radar, and performing menial tasks for pathetic wages simply don't afford. In addition, those who do cross the border illegally or who refuse to come forward to take advantage of this program can be reasonably assumed to have something to hide, and be subject to the consequences of detainment, incarceration, or deportation applicable to their proven offenses. The open border advocates can be happy, as can rule of law advocates.

We need immigration to continue in our prosperous ways. Taking away peoples of Latin and Arabic descent, America has more people leaving the workforce than it is replacing. It's no secret Arabs and Spanish peoples tend to have more children than homegrown American citizens; a fact stemming from religious views/practices, cultural differences, and more difficult demands on survival in less developed countries than that afforded by typical American comforts. I see it as a tremendous piece of foolishness for contemporary Republicans to not find a workable solution closer to the middle than their current entrenched position. If Republicans accomplish a compassionate *yet* accountable form of immigration, diminish their losses or even overtake the voting habits of Latinos, Arabs, and African-Americans (forgive the titillation, but more on that later), I don't know that they will ever lose another election.

Like I said above, this solution would require compromise on both sides, so let's all file it away under "P" for pipe dream.

Welfare

EVEN GREATER THAN our foreign aid and military budget is our welfare budget. I'm about to espouse some drastic changes to our welfare system, so those of you who are easily offended may want to take a smoke break and steel your spirit for a blushing crow. Those of you who have knee-jerk reactions to a conservative person advocating for the reduction of entitlements may want to throw this book in your fireplace without even finishing this sentence. I know it's a touchy subject whenever one talks about taking away entitlements. However, our government has swelled up to become a bloated, inefficient, corrupt abomination of a machine and continuing along its current path can only lead to implosion or continued suffering.

Lyndon Johnson and Franklin Delano Roosevelt had good intentions. What's more, they had tremendous resources to back up said intentions. Johnson was president during the height of the American car industry, all the industries which benefited from it, the height of the unskilled American worker, his family, the middle class, and by extension, government revenue. He had tremendous, indeed, unprecedented surpluses with which to work. His welfare system was an extension of Roosevelt's New Deal; a philosophy which stated that government should uphold the existence of the less fortunate. It was in response to these measures, and Johnson signing the Civil Rights Act, that the majority of African Americans began voting democrat. Johnson gave a famous speech at my beloved University of Michigan laying out his plan to use government resources to help others, stemming from a moral mandate to help those in need. I don't happen to personally believe that government is here to do as much as he said, but I don't fault his intentions or his actions. I do fault those who have let the system get out of hand. The conspiracy theorist in me urges the other me to believe they've actually pushed it along on this path. The other, other me is sick of being the only sane one in the room.

It's a clichéd truism, but times have changed. We no longer have GM, Ford, and Chrysler and their domino effect contributing to record government revenues. Detroit and Flint have gone from the richest *per capita* cities in the world to two of the poorest and most dangerous. Our government's financial standing has completely flip-flopped from where it was in Johnson's time. Not only does the government need to adjust its spending practices, but the welfare system needs to be updated to follow the model of encouraging people to be better versions of themselves. And just remember what I've already said, small as some of these changes might be, every little bit counts, and enough small changes will equal big improvements.

That's not to say that the welfare system is all bad. As I've stated, it was started with good intentions. It has kept many people afloat during times of trial. It has held the line between hardship and all-out catastrophe. But it has been corrupted, defrauded, and taken advantage of. It was never meant to be perpetual and generational. I am not wise enough to rank the presidents past Abraham Lincoln. I believe he's the best because he preserved our nation (albeit while giving up sovereignty of the states) and freed an entire race of people from bondage. Beyond that, I don't know that I could rank presidents based on the good they did. Permit me an irritated aside as I quite literally ask, can we just stop it with the idea that a good/ bad president is an on/off switch, okay? Just like two-fourths of the little people that issued from my bowels, presidents are on a spectrum. They have some winning ideas, policies, programs, decisions, and actions, and some losing ones. Pride over the last four-eight years of small victories and good ideas in my professional life is bound to be tempered by the mistakes and immoral judgments I make along the way (that is, if I'm a reasonable and intellectually honest person). Not a single one of them is all good and not a single one of them is all bad. Humans are too complex a creature to be categorically ranked in one of two moral judgment columns. Were we to destroy the stranglehold our two-party system has on politics, the idea of the other side's guys all being bad and our side's guys being all good would be a fortunate casualty. Were politicians to run on an individual platform, we'd lose so much of the tiresome rhetoric attached to this dogmatic support/dogmatic attacks.

However, based on the negative outcomes of Roosevelt and Johnson's programs, one could make the case for ranking Johnson as the worst. When it comes to the breakdown and weakening of families and negative effects on the poor of this country and how it has kept them from rising above their station, Johnson's program stands alone. Bear in mind, our country rejected the monarchy and the system which kept people in the class of their birth. Class mobility is a hallmark of our freedoms and opportunities. Because welfare appeals to our default setting of laziness and doesn't demand personal improvement, people on assistance tend not to improve. People raise or lower themselves to the expectations set and enforced for them.

Larry Elder doesn't mince words when talking about welfare. He states that in the 60's, officials canvassed the inner cities telling women of color that they had opportunity for government assistance so long as there wasn't a man in the house. In effect, he says, this allowed women to marry the government. This violates the idea of good intentions. It treads in agenda territory and is a reason I break from my conservative brothers and really believe in institutionalized racism. Replacing the husband and father with financial support silently implies that fathers are only good for an updated form of hunting and gathering. This reduction of the father's role to merely financial provider ignores the order, discipline, routine, leadership, moral instruction, and tender but firm love that come naturally to good men. Not to mention fathers being examples to young men on how to treat their wives with love, respect, attention, self-sacrifice, and affection. It's a travesty that the majority of children on assistance don't have this. What's more is that women continue to have children once they figure out that doing so leads to more money. Were I bolder, I'd say that having children so as to maximize welfare benefits metaphorically amounts to government sanctioned prostitution. But I'm not bold, so I won't put that thought into print. More and more children come into a fatherless situation and more and more of them miss out. Now, fathers wouldn't be marginalized if we didn't at first refuse to step up to our responsibility. However, society and government have changed so much that there is no incentive to involve fathers if a mother chooses not to. Here's what needs to change.

Make fathers a mandatory part of the equation. This is not difficult for two parent homes. They are already there and the household just needs assistance. In the majority of welfare homes, particularly the life-long and generational, fathers aren't in the home. We all know that some people just don't want to stay together. However, it is not the fault of the children that they didn't. Fathers and mothers need to work together to ensure a happy, healthy, responsible environment. Whether that takes place in the father's or the mother's home is immaterial. Unless dead or incarcerated, fathers should receive the financial assistance under the stipulation that they are accountable to the mother and the children to put in the necessary time each and every day raising the children. If they do not fulfill their obligation, the family unit should lose the assistance. Harsh, but necessary for change. Mothers can be given the means to hold the father accountable for the paying of bills and buying of necessities, and fathers can be given the means to hold the mothers accountable for making the children available for parenting, coming to and enforcing consistent rules, and getting the kids to school. Goodness, even the kids when they reach a certain age, can be given the means to hold both parents accountable for their respective and agreed-upon responsibilities, provided they are held accountable to going to school and achieving.

Cut assistance off at one child. This one won't be popular. I'm a reasonable guy and I know that families with multiple children have been given access to funds and become accustomed to this standard. Their children should be grandfathered in for the sake of not uprooting their lives. At some point the program needs to change permanently to only allow for one child for newcomers. Now, I don't believe in government-enforced sterilizations, as some conservatives do. That's barbaric and violates values of self-governance. But, it doesn't make any sense for the government to subsidize the continued irresponsibility of multiple children which can't be afforded. We all make irresponsible choices and mistakes. I had my first child at nineteen and for a brief period in my life filed for and was granted government assistance. But at the point where child after child is being born into assistance, it clearly is done on purpose. Logic has to return to its rightful place when judging the actions of those who take advantage of a system. It also contributes to generational assistance, which in turn creates generational poverty.

Generational poverty is in the same ballpark as slavery. Don't agree? When your life and continued existence is at the behest of a faceless entity that makes you jump through endless hoops in order to receive your subsistence, you've signed up for willful oppression. Oh, and they don't do it in a fast and caring manner. I've sat in the DHS office (Michigan's version of welfare) for eight hours waiting to see someone for ten minutes only to be told that I make too much money for a certain level of assistance. I've called my caseworker and never gotten a reply, only to have my assistance cut off because I missed a phone call (calling from a blocked number) from same caseworker. I've run around town frantically gathering paperwork so I can make it before the office closes for the weekend and my power being cut off. I've felt the anxiety and despair which comes from knowing that the government only cares about me if I put the right people into power. It's one reason why I can't in good conscience vote strictly vote democrat. Their welfare policies aren't truly helping Americans better their lives. I remember years ago when my parents had bailed my then-wife and me out financially for the second or third time in our young marriage, my sister remarked that they need to stop doing that. I wasn't offended but I was taken aback. Upon asking her why, she said that they aren't teaching me to be self-sufficient. By giving me an out, the next time I wanted to be irresponsible I would know I'd have an escape hatch if disaster struck. When I say the things in this book that are going to make me enemies, I say them to myself included. It wasn't until my wife left me and I won custody of my children that I learned better fiscal responsibility, and that only when circumstances demanded it. Necessity is the mother of invention.

All this does nothing to improve lives, and the government should have measures in place in order to force people to improve their lives and life station. Trust me; if a bold leader comes along and makes these major changes, we would see a drop in the number of fatherless children. The emperor has no clothes, everyone is just afraid to point it out.

Limit assistance to eight total years, consecutive or not. In the pragmatic sense, eight years is more than enough time to turn one's life around. And life ebbs and flows, so we should allow the Grover Cleveland non-consecutive paradigm on this one. This relates to what I said above. Government should make people improve. Under the current model, recipients of welfare have to *either* work a certain number of hours per week, *or* go to school. Here's the thing. The jobs they work aren't teaching marketable skills. They are typically hourly and unskilled labor, if at all. At Flint's local Work First office, recipients often sit there all day without being called for work, thereby fulfilling their requirement. If a recipient goes to school to learn a marketable skill and fails the schooling, they can just go back to the working option. Doing a little research shows that yes, this is a constant problem with recipients. It becomes a way to job the system, and there is little to no accountability or consequences for doing this. There is no reason to improve one's job skills and continue down the tracks to the next, nicer, more beautiful station.

In eight years, recipients can get two bachelor's degrees, four associate degrees, a bachelor's and two masters, six to eight certificates for wonderful jobs that require under or around a year of training, or a doctorate. And the government can make sure they are successful by making them repay for the schooling they fail, or cutting them off until it is repaid. You betcha britches we'd see real change in the system if people weren't given multiple means of escaping the responsibilities and burdens of adulthood. It will just take a fearless leader ready to make real change happen, the kind that will far outlast their presidency, not the kind of change that is quick, easy, and short term. In the game of golf, putting is important. But you can't play the short game without your drivers and woods doing their job first. Most presidents run on a platform of what they are going to accomplish in eight years. That's foolishness in this issue. It's time for America to start playing the long game.

One reason I can't in good conscience vote strictly republican is that they are too afraid to truly help. You are not truly helping a man when you don't help him better himself. They spend their time criticizing the democrats' programs but don't offer solutions. I see it as a fair accusation when democrats say that republicans don't care about the poor. I would just add as a caveat that neither party really, really cares about the poor. Otherwise real change would have already happened to this bloated and broken system. Democrats can't honestly say they care about the poor because they don't make the poor change things around. We've rejected the monarchy and rigid class systems here. Hence, we have class mobility. All it takes is some motivation, effort, and a few breaks. I entered adulthood with a baby and a working class wage. Through working like a madman, I entered the middle class by finishing college and starting my own business alongside my regular wage. Now I live comfortably and wouldn't even dream about considering the idea of maybe apologizing for the middle class wage I take home every year.

Limit the food available for purchase to essentials. I once collected WIC. It seems weird saying that because it stands for Women, Infants, and Children. But as a poor single father who had full custody of his kids, I was a stand-in for my children's mother, just as single mothers with custody are stand-ins for the fathers. Statistics show that single parent homes aren't ideal when measured against various metrics, but I take the view that I am going to play the cards I'm dealt, not the cards I desire. I believe the WIC model needs to be applied to welfare and food stamps. That is, restrictions on what can be bought. WIC allows for the purchase of milk, formula, eggs, peanut butter, juice, and a few other healthy and essential items. Food stamps allow for any food product. That is not only unethical, it is also terribly damaging. It's unethical because it allows for luxury items to be bought in lieu of essential items. This means the American taxpayer is being forced to subsidize luxury items. Make a statement like this in mixed company, and a progressive/social justice warrior/obnoxious person with no friends will immediately say "So, you're saying the poor don't deserve to have Doritos?!" or something along those lines. That's not it at all. Welfare is about survival, not luxury. Removal of luxury items from the roster should work as a motivation to get off assistance, or at least to work harder so as to be able to afford the occasional treat. Furthermore, the welfare system is filling the coffers of companies who flood the market with unhealthy food products. I don't know any reasonable person who would call this a societal good.

It's damaging because it adds to nation's health problems. There is a direct correlation between poverty and poor eating habits. The poor in lands of scarcity have a problem with finding food to eat. The poor in our country have a problem with the types of food they eat. This leads to all the related issues, including shorter lives full of poor health. As I have said before, the government should encourage and reward responsible behavior, not subsidize irresponsible. I've seen welfare recipients use their Bridge Card (Michigan's form of food assistance) buy oodles of pop, go around the corner, dump out the pop in the sewer, and return the bottles for money. If that's not abuse and fraud, I don't know that words make sense anymore. We all know the emperor has no clothes; it's just that everyone is afraid to speak up. If in charge, I'd even allow for a strictly limited number of treats. Problem is we don't even do that. I've even seen this idea argued against under the grounds that luxury foods don't make up a huge part of the money the government wastes. File this idea under the notion that in a country where the government spends far too much, every little bit saved helps.

Take away voting rights as a means of motivation. Do you hear that? It's the keyboards of the social justice warriors click-clacking away. SJW's don't tend to believe in gun ownership, so I'd say I'm safe from assassination...unless the upward trend of bow and arrow ownership since *The Hunger Games* burst onto the scene giving the finger to lesser YA literature options leads to a Smaug from *The Hobbit* (the diametric opposite of a lesser YA literature option) type death. In that case, avenge me, anyone who has the desire, the time, questionable morals, and a gun. They won't like this one but I'd ask everyone to hear me out. My dear reader should know by now that I'm all about personal responsibility, accountability, choices, rewards, consequences, and all that jazz. Yes, I can agree that it takes a village, to some extent. But the direction of one's life has more to do with one's individual choices than any other factor. And making choices that result in government assistance is something that should be understood and accepted, but not encouraged. And once it does happen, whatever can be done to encourage getting off it should be done. That might include some drastic measures.

When I was a child, my father worked at the Carriage Town Ministries in Flint. It's a now defunct charity program. He preached to crowds of homeless and poverty stricken who were there to get fed, and putting up with my dad's gospel sermon was a welcome trade in their eyes. Being a child of seven or eight, I mostly sat in the back and observed the proceedings. When the sermon was over, everyone lined up and got their meal. I remember my sister; as strong-willed a person as there ever was, resolutely telling adults many years older than she that "chocolate milk is for kids, and coffee is for adults!" as many of the adults came through the line and wanted chocolate milk. They left disappointed, having to face the brick wall that was Beth's resolve. Mind you, she was in the ten to twelve-years old range then. And she didn't lose, despite being cussed out, fussed at, and argued with. Now, did my sister make the decision that adults couldn't have chocolate milk? Of course not. She just enforced it.

That decision was made in whatever policy meeting involving the people who managed and operated the charity. Now, I wasn't there, but I can safely assume that the people lining up for their free food also weren't there. If they were, they may have voted for chocolate milk being given to adults. They may have argued that instead of a week, they should be given a bed for two months. They may have impressed upon the managers the need to give free cars away, along with stocking caviar and fine liquors in the kitchen. When you are entitled, there's no limit to what you can convince yourself you deserve from others. Here's the thing. People who rely on the charity of others shouldn't be allowed into the boardroom to make decisions. I know it sounds judgmental and harsh, but folks who have to have their existence sustained by loving people of means have, in some ways, excused themselves from the responsibilities of adulthood. This is, of course, leaving aside those who are physically or mentally unable to work. It shouldn't need to be said, but the exception to the rule is always what's brought up in debates of this sort. Our government should absolutely take care of these citizens. The overwhelming majority of citizens who are on assistance are there due to choices within their control, but aren't encouraged to change when they arrive in this situation. Taking away voting rights would do just that.

If I took a vote among my four children what they wanted to eat each and every night, they would almost always choose expensive foods that are bad for them, barring days that junk food has made them sick to their stomach. And, not having to pay for it, not seeing the hard work and struggle it takes me to earn the money to pay for it, they would continually vote in a self-centered way. They would do this until I either died, or was able to make them see the suffering they were causing. This would happen because they are children and children have to be taught to be other-centered. As I stated before, folks who perpetually accept assistance without a long term plan to get off it have excused themselves from the responsibilities of adulthood. What's more, they are not made privy to the struggles their enforced charity imposes upon taxpayers. Just as I don't make my nightly dinnertime a democratic process, and Carriage Town Ministries made their chocolate milk-withholding policy free of the influence of the people they are serving, just so should our government take away decision making power from Americans who rely on charity. They should be given assurances that they will be taken care of if they qualify, but not be allowed to have a say in choosing who will represent us in the lawmaking process.

Lest anyone accuse me of "dog-whistling", being a heterosexual Caucasian male of conservative bent and therefore unworthy of an opinion, or some such nonsense, remember a few things. There are more white people on welfare than black people. It'd be the height of foolishness to suggest that they all vote democrat. I know they don't all do it. I've got friends and coworkers on government assistance who kneel at the altar of Trump and possibly even offer up sacrifices of fruits, vegetables, and delectable meats (which the taxpayers paid for) at said altar. Most voters aren't single-issue voters. I'm talking about what would be expedient for our country to implement, not what is expedient for politicians. Furthermore, I had a baby at nineteen. I had to rely on the charity of family, friends, church, and government just to survive.

Not once did I look at the groceries people donated and say "Couldn't you have gotten Del Monte instead of Kroger Brand?" Not once did I take a $20 bill and sassily remark, "What, you can't make it $40?" When friends would fill up my gas tank so I could deliver pizzas that night and make it to whatever school I was subbing in and then to college classes the next day, not once did I ask them to go inside the station and grab me a Mountain Dew. Doing any of these things would have smacked of brazen and offensive entitlement, and certainly lost me some friends, along with subsequent help. Lest anyone accuse me of wanting this to happen so that only Republicans win elections, remember that I don't support that party. Welfare is typically associated with the Democratic platform, and was signed into law by a Democrat, but Republicans are just as much to blame for the current state of affairs as Democrats. I actually formulated this idea of taking away voting rights when I was on welfare. I knew that if I didn't have a say, I would get off it faster. And so will most people. Having a voice is a powerful thing in the psyche and confidence of an individual.

Philosophically speaking, one could make the argument that welfare is not even charity. Charity is love and assistance given willingly with a pure heart, clean motives, and no expectation of return beyond the emotional satisfaction that comes when helping someone in need, usually triggered by their thanks and gratitude. Government-enforced charity as part of your individual tax burden on account of earned wages is no charity at all because it is none of those things. Taxpayers don't give it of their own accord. They don't see, interact, and associate with the people who receive it, so they can't humanize and love them on a personal level. It's done with the motives of government, and only God knows what those are from day to day. There is no emotional satisfaction as there is little to no thanks coming in from those who receive it. I've seen people flippantly say "You're welcome" to welfare recipients in the grocery store checkout lane. That's problematic enough as it's quite rude and calls attention to an embarrassing subject. However, I've never once seen a welfare recipient get on any platform and sincerely thank taxpayers for their charity. Rather the opposite, I've seen welfare recipients interviewed and talk about how they should get more, and are going to vote in those who will maintain or increase entitlements. That's like a kick to the nuggets when you're trying to block one to the teeth. Welfare in its current form is as far from real charity as the East is from the West. Food for thought. Chew on it and see if it agrees with you.

Understand and redefine this as an American problem. A recent statistic I read states 35% of welfare recipients are white and 25% are black. Race-baiting liberals would say that it's unfair for welfare to be a black stereotype because more white people are on it.

I'd agree, it most certainly is unfair. Race-baiting conservatives (yes, there are plenty despite "race-baiting" being a typical conservative pejorative) would say that for 13% of the population, 25% is disproportionately high, and 35% coming from 70% of the population is disproportionately low. As you might glean from my writing, there are inside me a compassionate liberal and line-in-the-sand conservative always at war. They both seem nonplussed by the kid in me who enjoys the caramelized sugar side of Frosted Mini Wheats. Sad truth is that the race baiters on both sides can't see the forest for the trees. Besides engaging in racial and class rhetorical warfare, they are arguing minutia and missing the big point. They both tend to separate the black community from America writ large. This is not a black, white, puce, fuchsia, or rainbow colored problem. If you only get one thing from this book, make it the next sentence. What's bad for the black community *is bad for America*. The measures I've proposed above will take black and white people off generational welfare and force race-baiters on both sides to find a new subject to argue, which I'm sure they will.

Conclusion (of this section, you've got more to read, if you dare) Some of the measures I propose above would make the leader who enacts them even more of a target for assassination. That's fine. Risk is part of the job. What would be (and probably is) even worse is that proposing some of these harsh measures would make them unelectable. We have done some things for so long we see them as non-negotiable. That's foolishness in my eyes. Beyond moral stances, I don't see that the temporal structures we set up here on earth shouldn't be up for compromise. I believe that the Lord of Heaven has vouchsafed my reward beyond this life. But what I do in this life (if I don't violate His clear boundaries) is always on the table. What's more, we are handing a bill to our issue that they will not be able to pay, no matter how exceptional they turn out to be. A president who slashes spending but keeps taxes consistent, or even raises them for a limited amount of time, should be able to cut our deficits and set precedents which will allow our issue to eliminate them. I was raised by and around staunch Republicans. When it comes to judging Bill Clinton as a president many, as you would rightly assume, did so strictly down party lines. What they don't remember or refuse to acknowledge is that he cut spending and left his successor with a surplus. I still remember cashing the six hundred dollar check George W. Bush sent to me and my young bride early in his presidency as part of a stimulus package that came from said surplus. Unless someone comes along and takes drastic measures, history will have no choice but to remember Clinton as the last president to be fiscally sound enough to do such a thing, on top of being a really wicked sax player...and those other unsavory things he did.

Healthcare

AAAHHH THE EARLY presidency of George W. Bush. Those were the days. A good cross-section of the country was better with words than their president. The crack/heroin/marijuana/crystal meth on steroids cocktail that is the smartphone wasn't on the market yet. Social media was in its infancy and people didn't try to ruin the lives of total strangers when other total strangers of questionable integrity and motives told them they should hate this other total stranger. I actually got through reading a book without letting myself get constantly distracted. DVD's were still a thing and had utterly trounced the arrogant upstart laserdiscs. The Lord of the Rings was paving the way for fantasy movies of the comic book persuasion down the road. Leroy Jenkins and the monkey passing out from sniffing its finger after digging in its butt were the only two viral videos. And Democrats found another entitlement in the form of universal healthcare snugly hidden away in the Constitution.

At least, that's when this idea came on my radar. It made sense. For many years, people had sued doctors and hospitals to the point that where it was even possible to practice medicine, malpractice insurance rates were so high that doctors, out of a sense of self-preservation, had settled into a routine of stacking patient appointments one on top of the other so as to maximize their billable time and giving everyone as many painkiller medications and Cesarean section deliveries they demanded, no matter the long term consequences. Now, I'd be a fool to think that the millions of people who have sued doctors in the age of unchecked litigation are liberal, but I'd also be a fool to think that the majority of people who believe in suing the rich whenever a mistake (real or perceived) is made aren't liberal. The folks who constantly preach about earning your keep and letting the wealthy keep their...keep are the same ones who typically are sparingly litigious and not frivolously so. Far be it from me to throw criticism without offering a solution (after all, I'm not an elected Washington D.C. official or rabid Twitter user), so here we go.

Define the types of malpractice and standardize the amount allowed for each type. I know there are some bad doctors out there, just like every other industry. I know there are some corrupt ones who engage in criminal malpractice. The justice system can take care of the criminal part of their misdeeds. The really bad doctors are typically weeded out through market correction and media scrutiny. The ones who make a mistake here and there should be given the leeway to be considered human. I understand that when a doctor makes a mistake, the stakes are higher than when my son doesn't do every step in long division on a math worksheet or when I cut a lawn a tad crooked. But they are still human. We rely on them to help us in an hour of need. Many times, they make an honest mistake. If tort reform and litigation were limited across the board as to what you can claim from your doctor's insurance, their insurance rates would go down. Lower rates for insurance would mean lower service rates for doctors, which would in turn make them better at deliberate and personal customer service, maybe even the triumphant return of (gasp) house calls for those of us not part of the super-rich 1% (knee-jerk hissing and booing noise appropriate at this point).

Formulate and practice a reward system for doctors who do their job despite the cost in customers. I have suffered on and off again with back problems since I was twenty-two years old. A slip and fall accident on my porch coupled with years of bad posture, backbreaking work, and poor weight and strength management have all factored into it. Like many folks, I disregard the AMA's propaganda against chiropractors and have made many visits to several different of these wonderful dudes. It wasn't until I visited my fourth chiropractor that I was informed that they don't need to take X-rays, they don't need to see you multiple times a week, and they shouldn't be trying to sell you massage equipment. The chiropractor I visit now says that contrary to common practice, a chiropractor can feel what is wrong with your back without X-rays (so don't ever shell out $90 for X-rays again), you should visit them when *you* need to visit them (multiple weekly visits actually having the adverse effect of making you dependent on them instead of strengthening your back on your own), and selling massage equipment is an unnecessary measure to just make some extra scratch on the side. I had no idea until I met one with a larger measure of professional integrity. And he backed his words up with the best chiropractic work I've ever experienced. This man has a smaller practice, fewer customers coming in at regular intervals, and makes no money on the side selling Swedish massage chairs. But he has integrity and a loyal customer in me.

Same with a lot of general practice doctors. Zachary Lemon; a good friend from high school and fellow author, describes how he deals with difficult and entitled customers. When they demand pills for a problem that can be solved with a lifestyle change, he makes sure they know a lifestyle change could fix the problem while the pills would only be treating the symptom, and politely encourages them to find another doctor if they are displeased with what he has to tell them. Due to the nature of the typical American patient, he's limited in the people he'll eventually serve in his career, but unlimited in the profound help he can render his little slice of the population. It is this type of doctor who sticks to their guns, working in conjunction with government incentivizing personal discipline in health management, which could have a transformative effect on the industry. Doctors already have tremendous oversight for their work. A government sponsored system which gives them an added motivation to conduct their business with integrity could easily be put in place.

As a start, make free all life-saving medications. Democrats know so many things. They are always telling the population how much smarter they are. One thing they know of a certainty is that prescription drug companies are evil. I am riding the fence in this debate. Drug costs have skyrocketed in the same era that doctor costs have. I'm not wise enough to spot the correlation or determine the causation, nor will I try. I also know that companies are in the business of turning a profit and they have a right to do just that. I think a decent compromise for a government that wants to find a good middle ground between increasing entitlements to all Americans and curtailing market abuses by the companies is to find a way to make drugs that are needed for the continuation of life free for diabetic, cancer, and other types of patients. Once that's achieved, it might be possible to find a happy medium for those drugs that, if taken, dramatically increase one's quality of life and capacity for productive work. Slow down, tweakers, I'm not talking pain medication. I'm talking about blood thinners and other chemical agents which help an aging body function more properly.

I don't advocate for universal healthcare, at least in the form that it has taken in many socialist countries. It's clear that the quality of care can and often does suffer in such places. United Arab Emirates is a wonderful example of universal care done right. It's difficult to compare to America though, as that's a tiny nation with a miniscule population that is sitting on an ocean of crude. Oil, that is. Black gold. Texas tea. Arabian coffee. Vehicular *haema*. I'll stop now. Point is, our government isn't exactly flush with cash right now, nor are they going to seize and control all oil sales and distribution anytime soon, Venezuela's current turmoil being a good example of what not to do in a similar situation.

Universal care is a wonderful dream but not feasible as we currently stand. If we slash spending and cut deficits, we can talk, and we should talk. Universal care could then become the privilege of a once again wealthy nation. I don't agree that it's the fundamental right of every American citizen though. As I've said before, will say in the future, and will repeat right here, once you've adopted the entitlement mentality, there's no limit to what you can convince yourself you deserve at the cost of others. Problem is, there's no free lunch.

Offer a government option with government employees. Obama had lofty goals when he offered universal healthcare. That and his skill in windsurf-ing made him the coolest president since Coolidge. The execution is where things got messy. Mountains of books, blogs, vlogs, tweets, and watercooler argu-ments have been composed on this topic, so I'll spare my two cents and save for my kid's college. What they did wrong is instead of offering a government service provider option, they just offered coverage. Many people couldn't find a doctor who would accept the coverage, and prices for care and prescription drugs were adversely affected.

The CIA, FBI, and U.S. military recruit kids right out of high school and college who precisely fit their respective services. The USPS offers a cheap service which is comparable to their newer private-sector competition. Very few government programs have pri-vate-sector counterparts. Healthcare should be added to that list.

Think about the benefits. We all know the USPS is fast and efficient because it is a value-added gov-ernment service with fierce competition. What if the government recruited young doctors out of medical school, offered them a reasonable wage commen-surate with the cheapened government coverage, guaranteed their malpractice insurance coverage in terms of honest mistakes (barring gross negligence, incompetence, or criminality), oversaw their practice and professional behavior, and encouraged them to practice in underprivileged areas, like the inner cities, rural areas, and South Carolina, where hucksters like John Edwards made their fortunes suing doctors out of the state. The Fed could even offer perks like repayment of their college debts for staying on the payroll for a certain number of years and not going private.

In a reversal of the process that happened with UPS and FedEx, doctors on the government rolls could build practices, clinics, and reasonably sized hospitals in competition with older, more experienced, and more costly doctors and hospitals, and the people who can afford such services would be left happy to do so, while the poor among us would have a more affordable option. Certainly the more costly doctors would lose customers who only care about the bottom line cost, but that's where my other plans above for the industry will make it possible for them to lower prices, and maintain quality while still remaining competitive and viable. Yes, there will be an adjustment for everyone. Fewer doctors will enter private practice, and some may even be put out of business. But humans have this uncanny habit of adapting to hard times and thriving after they've got it figured out. Doctors are necessary and helpful to society, but they are first and foremost private business owners. They know there are risks involved with starting and maintaining one's small business.

Something to make both sides of the aisle happy, you say? While I curtail my enthusiasm, you go ahead and file this idea under "F" for fantasy fiction.

Crime

I DON'T KNOW if you are a human being with working eyes and functional ears, and have not been off-planet for the last like, forever years, but humanity does some bad stuff to each other. America is no exception. In fact, we are leaders (good to be number one in something, am I right?) in crime compared to many other countries. Liberals and Conservatives have some good and bad ideas, as I've stated before. Sometimes, good ideas from both sides can be combined to form something new. It has to be said that no race, color, creed, religion, or any other human grouping is running a monopoly on wickedness, nor is any of these groupings innocent on all parts. Liberals who scream about the rate of mass shootings perpetrated by white men and conservatives who scream about the rate of one-on-one violence perpetrated by black men aren't accomplishing anything. Both are huge problems, on top of all the other crime we have to deal with. Dividing it by race or color does nothing but keep us divided and easily controlled by those we vote into power.

Conservatives say that when a person removes themselves from the social contract, breaks the rules of civilization, and transgresses natural or legislated law, they should be punished. I agree. They should pay a debt to society. Problem is our prison system is such a money-making machine that it's been corrupted to do nothing about the staggering rates of incarceration, particularly of those who come from low socioeconomic backgrounds. Helping these poor souls either before or after they commit a crime is lost in the cogs and gears of the machine.

Liberals levy the money-making criticism, the high incarceration rates and imbalanced sentences among black males criticism, and the idea that the poor are forced into committing crimes by our rigged system. I agree with the first two, not so much with the last, but I understand it. Conservatives will argue that no one is "forced" to commit crimes. I would say the same thing with the caveat that if someone is not raised with even a shred of morality relating to the idea of neither harming, nor picking the pocket of their fellow man, they will have no qualms about doing such. So for me, this part of the argument comes to values, morality, and personal choices. Many people who abide by the law are aware of it, but only the potential consequences constrain them, morality does not.

Liberals also say that we should adopt some of

the prison practices of eastern Europe, particularly the Nordic countries. There, rehabilitation and inculcation into society are the primary goals. Conservatives say that this treats the criminal better than the victim, that the Nordic countries are too small and homogenous to apply their practices here, and that a lot of criminals deserve to rot in a cell. Liberals and conservatives are all too ready to dismiss an idea out of hand, penciling in the reasons why along the way. Clearly our current privatized prison system of three hots and a cot for a set amount of time isn't working. Like conservative commentators, I believe in consequences, but also second chances. I've found in my own life, though I've never engaged in criminal activities (unless you count being criminally handsome), that life is full of second, third, fourth, eightieth, and one thousand and fifty fourth chances. The only chance that is final is one stemming from a choice that results in loss of life, limb, or ability. Maybe we can combine the goals of consequences, rehabilitation, and inculcation into something better than what we have. Once combined, these ideas will join up and stop intergalactic crime in the form of Voltron; Defender of the Universe, swinging a mighty, mystical sword of justice and bringing…(editor's note: this joke has run its course).

Educate prisoners better than we are. This is being done to some extent, but it's not satisfactory in my eyes, because many criminals get out of jail and go back to their life of crime. This has also to do with factors I bring up later, but it has a lot to do with their personal skill set.

Leaving aside the brilliant kingpins of crime like Pablo Escobar, Kenneth Lay, the Cali Cartel, the Illuminati, Walter White, and Wilson Fisk, talk to a petty criminal and take an inventory of their intelligence. Most of them cannot read, write, communicate, reason, and think critically on an adult level. This stems from not doing their due diligence in school, the environment of the schools they attended, poor examples in their lives, chaos counterproductive to learning and lack of education at home, and unfit educators. This is where the obnoxious conservatives come in. They are fond of making statements beginning with "Well, they should have...". Whether or not they should have made better choices as a young person is at this point immaterial. They didn't, and continually pointing it out doesn't accomplish anything, nor does it mitigate the fact that a criminal who has paid their debt deserves a second chance at life. Shame on any conservative who believes someone doesn't deserve gainful employment and cautious (at first) trust when reentering society.

Prisons make education available. I say we make it compulsory, and attaining an education a condition of release. Not only an education, but a marketable skill, or multiple marketable skills. Many young people, young men especially, get out of a high school that barely taught them, unequipped to go to college, lacking in the skills necessary to get ahead. More often than not, they choose to either steal from others or get into the drug game. The reasons are simple. There's a promise of good money with minimal work, along with acceptance into a group of supposedly loving adults. No rational person can minimize the power of acceptance. Those promises outweigh the dangers in their minds. We as humans not only continually calibrate towards comfort, but also the path of least resistance in the direction of accomplishing goals. It's no wonder we are at the point that many of their moms and liberals continually make excuses for these young people, telling the rest of us that they are "forced" to commit crimes to survive. The verbiage is wrong but the rationale is sound, even if it's immoral. Someone might feel "forced" when they see the easiest way out. It can be the duty of civilized folk to show them where they went wrong and how they can do better next time.

Young people who made poor decisions in school but want to go to college are forced into community college, essentially paying to learn what they should have learned in secondary school for free. Young people who made poor decisions in school and get into crime get three hots and a cot, often a terrible prison culture of violence, anger, gangs, rape, and other stress factors, and not much else. Fundamentally changing themselves as people in prison is more difficult than just surviving until their release date. Maybe more accurately, surviving until their release makes anything else nigh unto impossible. I've seen it as a teacher. We educators say that "failure is not an option" but we fail to follow through. I've seen young men sit with their head in their hands all day long, sleep through classes, do little to no work, accept the free lunch and leisure time we award for just being there, and then go home. They are doing the same as a prisoner who just survives until his release. Failure is an option to them and we educators give them multiple means to fail without harsh consequences. It's one of the many reasons I send my kids to a private school, but that's a discussion for another chapter.

Once a prisoner has undergone the necessary training to read, write, and communicate, reason, and solve problems, they should be given access to either college or trade courses. Completion, apprenticeship, and practice of their chosen trade should be a condition of release, no matter the crime. This could be a time when they choose something they have experience and aptitude in, or something completely new. I think we as a society would be pleasantly surprised to find out just how dramatically prisoners turn themselves and their lives around when only given one way out. Certainly, they are prisoners, and are living in a prison. They aren't there for farting in church, and they aren't at the four seasons, but that doesn't mean they need to suffer at all points. Actually showing compassion, forgiveness, and giving second chances to those who have messed up is a vital practice in education, parenthood, business, and that one thing... what's it called...oh yeah, life. Most importantly, these guys should be trained to be safe, responsible, and law-abiding adults. If you want to throw at me "They should know how to be an adult" I can agree, but would say that if you had a good childhood you'd be shocked and surprised at the extreme nature of what many went through as children. They at one point excused themselves from the rules of civilization, or never learned them to begin with. I believe they should be given the training and chance to earn their way back in. We'd have fewer problems in the long run if we spend the time and money to do this.

Just because they have messed up a little bigger than those on the outside doesn't mean they don't deserve compassion. I differ from most Republicans on this account. I think this kind of measure should be undertaken even for those serving life sentences that can show themselves capable of living within a civilized prison society. To me, that man or woman has an everlasting soul, stamped on them in the image of God; something that has built-in dignity and is deserving of respect. Rehabilitation should always be a goal, whether or not that man will ever breathe free air again. You might be helping to save a soul and help the next generation avoid the mistakes of the current. Do a little research on the Son of Sam and his remarkable story once his prison sentence began. I think you'll see what I mean, even if you don't agree. Once again, the exception to the rule must be addressed. There are those individuals so deranged and dangerous that merely having them around other people triggers their crazy. It's difficult to help them and train them to be better human beings. My simple answer there is prayer, maybe a little compassion at arm's length with proper restraints in place. Who knows? I can't solve every problem here.

Make prisoners pay their debt not only to society, but to the victims. We make prisoners wait out a sentence. This is justice according to our system. But we don't always make them repay their victims. Victims and families have to enter the civil court system in order to start this process. This, as a condition of release, will not only encourage prisoners to pay their debt, but might even constrain those considering committing a crime. You've made yourself personally responsible to increase the comfort of those you've harmed. Taking a life, ruining a life, stealing from someone, etc. all can be devastating to an individual and their loved ones. However, time and financial relief can help them heal. I feel dirty even saying this, but a standardized monetary amount of money should be applied to every crime, and that amount paid to victims and survivors by felons hoping to attain release. We do make prisoners work in prison, but mostly in ways that drive up prison revenue. This should remain in place for prisoners who either are new and haven't gotten skills yet, or for those who step out of line and need remediation. Once a prisoner has gained a skill, they should be given work release opportunities to earn wage; all of which can go to victims and their families until their debt is paid. Obviously, standards should be set and consistently applied no matter the status of the criminal, or the location the crime occurred. One thing I can't stand in our current system is that people can buy easier sentences with high-priced lawyers, or get off easier based on the place they committed the crime. I count that a vulgar thing, and it's led to statistics suggesting that non-whites are judged more harshly. Maybe the federal government stepping in and superseding the states in this capacity would be advisable.

Be more aggressive in expunging records. My dear friend and former business partner Johnny makes a good point when referencing his sordid past. He committed crimes in his twenties. He was caught. He was sentenced. He served his sentence. At some point, he was enticed by old contacts to get back in the game. Upon his release, he made the conscious choice to not get back into the game. He is now in his mid-forties. He works hard, earns, takes care of his own, and pays his taxes. And yet he still can't get certain jobs. That's because his government record still shows that he's a criminal (maybe not in verbiage, but definitely in effect) and can't be trusted because of mistakes he made in the flower of manhood. Basically, something you do when you're young and dumb stays with you your entire life and you're always judged for it in the business sense, if not others.

Someone who follows the path I've suggested above should have their record expunged, completely, fully, utterly, and to the utmost. Probationary periods and precautionary methods can still apply. But at some point, they should be given a fresh start and a clean slate. Who among us is the same person at the age of forty-five as we were at twenty-five, or fifteen (when most criminal lives start)? If you are, I feel sorry for you. If you've grown and changed as a person, bully for you. If you've devolved and regressed as a person, it's never too late to improve. I understand there are some crimes that stem from addiction, chemical imbalances, and home environments during the formative years AND harm others, like rape and pedophilia. A happy middle ground (like increased monitoring, managing, administering, and control over their civilian life) can be found in most instances, and on a case-by-case basis, not a cookie-cutter, one-size-fits-all, blanket standard. But someone who dealt drugs as an adolescent for quick cash, beat up a sexual rival in a moment of high passion, crashed a car after a night of carousing, or basically showed poor judgment as a youth should be given every available chance to show they've changed, improved, and will never do it again. I have made many mistakes in my life, and I thank God above that the foolishness of my youth, my early adult years, and my midlife years aren't going to be held against me for all my life.

Despite the nature of some crimes, I can't be sold the idea that anyone is beyond redemption, either behind bars or in front of them. Many violent men and women in prison have tested the boundaries of man's depravity. Some extremes so heinous they must stay imprisoned. But an implicit logic behind the phrase "pay one's debt to society" demands that their record is clean once they've paid that debt. I don't continue to get annoying collection calls once I've cleared my Columbia House account. I still order CD's through the mail. Don't judge me. I shouldn't harass someone out of prison because they've been punished for stepping outside of our laws and paid for it. I look at the terrible deeds of some champions of my faith and how they were redeemed from them and I can't say that anyone is beyond redemption. And yes, liberals, that also means that racists, homophobes, and those intolerant of transgendered people aren't beyond redemption. Careful guys! You're liable to knock something over with all that indignant scoffing.

This viewpoint of crime stems from my faith. Call my faith what you like. But it is above all else, a faith of redemption from sin. One cannot be redeemed if they do not sin, or if someone in a position over them does not forgive and redeem them. The Bible is a lot of things to a Christian like me. It is a volume of history, narrative, poetry, conflict, praise, worship, doctrine, warnings, and prophecies. It is not just one of those things. All of these things coalesce into making it what it really is; a story of redemption from sin. The overall message of the Bible is that man is sinful, in need of redemption, and can be redeemed through the work of a saviour. How can I believe in eternal redemption for the soul when I don't believe in redemption for the body which houses that soul? I think my ideas can be adopted and practiced by conservatives and liberals alike.

If I'm wrong, I'll accept the decision of the court.

Make a moral stance and personal statement of faith a condition of release. It's been said that legislation can't change hearts, but laws can constrain the heartless. I believe it to be true. Many people only stop themselves from harming others based on the potential reckoning coming from the law once they break the social contract. All the education in the world won't change an evil heart. Nazi-controlled Germany was one of the most educated societies in the world. We all know how that worked out. The measures I posit above are pragmatic in nature. I want a debt to the betrayed society be paid, and victims to be recompensed to ease, maybe even heal their suffering. But these measures don't address the criminal's soul.

Whether or not a prisoner maintains their innocence throughout their stay, they need to take measures of self-improvement to make sure they don't ever go back. This includes either adopting a faith or at the very least, a moral economy. Studies in faiths of all nature and comparative religions should be enforced and prisoners should be made to come up with a personal statement of morality and letters of redressing wrong to their victims and families. Even if they choose the atheistic and materialistic way of life, they should be made to state why, according to that worldview and its social constructs, what they did was wrong and why it was wrong, and what they are doing to make sure it is not going to happen again.

This seems like something a high school would do to poorly behaved children. And that is true. High schools do it to make children reflect on their behavior. Reflection offers the chance for the process of shame, guilt, regret, apology, and quest for forgiveness to do their work on the child's spirit and soul. Just as I've mentioned several times up to this point, criminals who prey upon others have removed themselves from the rules of civilization. In a way, they have acted as foolish children. They need to show society and their peers that they can be brought back. Picking a moral standard and planting their flag gives the chance for them to see, according to whatever moral standard they adopt, why what they did was wrong and work on self-applied principles to avoid it in the future, not just out of fear of reprisal and consequences. It's amazing to me that we enforce reflection on our children, students, leaders and members of societal groupings, politicians, even employees, but don't even encourage convicted felons to engage in this process. Reflection is a powerful tool, beyond the fact that a contrite heart is one not guided by pride. Once out of the pen, the people overseeing their transition back into society can be members of the faith/worldview they've adopted. This will give reformed convicts a chance to learn from and be mentored by someone wiser in the faith than they. Some might call this planting a seed and encouraging the increase. We can do this even if someone maintains their innocence. They can still make a statement of faith and say why the crime for which they received sentence was wrong and must be avoided.

Have government incentives for staying out of trouble. I've said it before and I'll say it again. Government should incentivize moral behavior, not just punish immoral behavior. Whenever government incentivizes and subsidizes a certain behavior, it automatically gets more of it. A deduction in taxes I'm suggesting is for people who don't get tickets, misdemeanors, and crimes. We should have a predetermined amount of time in place to incentivize a reformed convict who can take advantage of this deduction once they've shown they can keep their nose clean. Easy peasy. This will discourage recidivism and encourage getting into and plying their trade. Changing lives. It's not what I get paid to do, but it's what I enjoy doing the most.

Create family jails. Oooh boy, this one will stick in some craws. It's no surprise that teenagers who engage in petty crime continue in more serious criminal activity as adults. Juvenile detention centers, on top of being a laughing stock for their lenient sentences, have the same type of toxic environments as adult prisons. It shouldn't be a controversial statement to say that juveniles who commit crimes do so partly out of fault of their parents. Lack of discipline, structure, and moral training all lead up to this in the years when parents absolutely can and should control their children. If we force mothers and fathers of adolescents to serve time with, and indeed, in the same prison cells as their troubled youth, we'd see a drastic drop off in absentee fathers and apathetic mothers, and an increase in cooperation to ensure proper upbringing, primarily among those who have split up. The potential loss of freedom, employment, housing, and time away from children who aren't committing crimes would serve as a stern reminder of the consequences to letting difficult children run wild. I've said many times that consistent parenting is difficult, permissive parenting is easy. Children whose parents aren't consistent in the formative years more often than not have to put up with insufferable teenagers. This seems like a perfect time to get their act together before they release these young people to an unsuspecting world. As an added bonus, I may have just stumbled upon an idea for an entertaining reality television show.

Force prisoners to create working, efficient communities for themselves. As a teacher, I have found that students want tasks and ownership of their classroom. They thrive in such a situation because ownership and accepted tasks invoke a feeling of purpose. As far as I understand, prisoners who behave themselves are allowed to work as janitors, cooks, and in various other roles. They are given time out of their cells for meals and yard activities. We don't make them work together for survival though. We don't make them grow their own food, form and join positive groups, assign roles, elect leaders, develop and maintain social skills, hold each other accountable, and support each other. It's no wonder gangs and the gang mentality are formed and maintained in prisons. It's no wonder prisoners separate themselves by race and spend time intimidating and harming others. We know they lack in the skills civilization needs from them, but we don't teach them these skills, nor make it beneficial for them to do so. And we wonder why repeat offenders are such a problem.

I believe that once the government starts looking to the problems in its own house and allocates funds previously given to other countries and other programs, our urban centers will start to clean up themselves. This, combined with an overhaul of our prison paradigm will lower our crime rate. Crimes will still happen, certainly. And we can't expect to reach and save 100% of criminals. We can, however, expect to save more than we currently are, especially in communities wracked by crime. We can enter an age in which responsibility and morality is the norm, not the exception. It will take a while, yes. But I've already addressed the idea that we should be playing the long game, not the short game. Pragmatically changing quickly for immediate, measurable results often does harm in the long run. I may not have to point it out to my more observant readers, but this would make the title of my book quite ironic, or at least sarcastic. Feel free to chuckle now.

Reparations

DO YOU HEAR that? The ultra conservative keyboard warriors are cracking their knuckles and limbering up to make sure they don't pull a hammy furiously crafting an indignant response to this one. Hopefully my logic and appeal to Biblical authority will sway a few to this side.

This is a touchy subject. It's touchy for conservative white people. That means that most liberal whites and persons of color don't care how touchy it is. White and black conservative commentators ascribe the epithet "victim Olympics" to those who seek reparations and other recompense for past or current injustices. In the victim Olympics, white people are dead last, at least in this country. Caucasians really aren't allowed to celebrate collective victories, nor are they allowed to cry out in collective offense. It's okay though. Many white folks have done okay in this country. Just look at the outdated colonial, expansion, and frontier laws for land ownership. In addition, some of the baser among them get back in a passive-aggressive manner by attributing collective embarrassment whenever a person of color makes a bad showing of being a decent human being. I think one way to fix racial tension is for everyone to stop doing all three of these things, but that's an argument for another book.

The descendants of Africa, more than any other group of people, have suffered at the hands of this country. The final clause in the first amendment in our sacred Bill of Rights allows every citizen to "petition the Government for a redress of grievances". Have grievances been redressed? The freeing of slaves didn't do that, as it only gave to them what was supposed to be assumed, guaranteed, and inalienable to all people of this land. The starting point for redress is farther down the road. Civil rights didn't do that. It recognized black Americans as full citizens, something they should have had since the beginning if recognized legally (as they already did practically) as being in possession of full personhood. Once again, something was given to them that others of different races didn't have to fight for. I see no redress of grievances so far. Some of my philosopher friends feel that if you're going to talk about reparations to the descendants of slavery, you should talk about reparations to the descendants of those who fought to end slavery. This symmetrical argument is perfectly fine with me, but it is too often used as a refutation of black reparations, not as a wholly justified "while you're at it, can you also..." I see no problem with a similar kind of measure for descendants fitting that description, but we first need to start talking about how to do this.

Now, I'm no progressive or social justice warrior. When I hear activist groups talking about the 1%, clamoring for the redistribution of wealth, and basically causing a ruckus instead of going to work, my calm and collected answer is that wealthy folks who earned their money honestly and ethically have every right to disperse or hoard their wealth in any means they wish within the confines of the law. And those born into those families who do absolutely nothing to earn said wealth have the right to accept it when daddy and mommy pass it on to them. Like it or not, it's not really unfair, in terms of the dictionary definition of the word. I despise the idea of rich kids inheriting wealth simply by being born with the right last name, but I also despise the idea of government stealing people's stuff because a loud contingent refuse to work for their own lump of wealth.

But, I'm also not terribly in line with many conservatives. They are quick to point out that Japanese were interned during Dubya-Dubya Two, and that Japanese are doing well on the global business stage. Plus, they get all the best Nintendo games before they come to the U.S. markets. Lucky jerk-faces. They are quick to point out that Jews have fared well here, despite a long history of oppression, Diaspora, and overall discomfiture. They are quick to point out that other Asian cultures, Kenyans, and Arabs all do well here, and that African-Americans just need to get with the program and stop whining. They are quick to point out that slavery happened a long time ago, that Africans were slave traders, that certain sports and much of pop culture is dominated by blacks, and that we had a black president. All somewhat valid responses. But allow me to retort point. by. blessed. point. Whoops, sorry for that. Let me get you a tissue. Enunciating my bilabial plosives often results in spitting a little bit.

Japanese internment wasn't even on the same scale of suffering that slavery was. While this may not be comparing apples to oranges, it's certainly comparing apples to apple seeds. Next, Jews were never, ever, never, ever, neeeeevvver systematically oppressed here in America. They emigrated here *en masse* in the late 1800's and early 1900's when they saw opportunity, some of them coming because they were no longer welcome in their home countries. Watch *Fiddler on the Roof* for a fictional portrayal of this based on real history of the horrific pogroms which occurred. They came here and formed communities to help each other and they came here with modern education and skills that helped them get ahead as they formed these communities.

That last sentence doesn't apply to Africans. They had their communities and families torn apart. Folks convinced themselves, their children, friends, and their government that they were less than human and unworthy of a voice, education, and the basic privileges afforded by families held together. Family is the last temporal line of defense against calamity, the most comforting salve when calamity strikes, and the strongest ally of prosperity. The argument I made of the Jews joining the melting pot rings similarly true to all the other races I mentioned above. They all came here of their own accord and with resources backing them up. Now we really are in apples and oranges territories.

Slavery happened a long time ago. True enough. But civil rights weren't granted until the 1960's. That's one hundred years of not being recognized as a full human being and not being afforded basic inalienable rights. What's more, (the following idea gleaned from my good friend Russell Andrews-El, who factors later into one of my book's rambling personal anecdotes) civil rights really aren't divine rights. The opening paragraph to the Declaration of Independence makes clear what divine rights are. It even argues that government may not take away rights endowed by our Creator. Christians, Catholics, Orthodox Jews, and Muslims, and many eastern religions all believe in an eternal soul; the image of God. This image is the only part of us that is everlasting, existing beyond the death of the fleshly vessel. My friend states that before civil rights, divine rights should have been recognized for the descendants of Africa. Civil rights, while valuable, mainly dictated the legal manner in dealing with public discourse and privileges, interaction, fair trade, and political action. Divine rights see the person as a complete equal without allowing for any limiting qualifiers based on any external factor you can possibly imagine. Civil rights cannot hold or precede divine rights but can and do spring naturally out of the recognition of divine rights.

Cracker, tell me that can happen to you and your people and it not affect your collective psyche. To this day, black people who lived through the 30s, 40s, and 50s (men especially) look at the ground, avoid eye contact, and answer white people with "yes sir" and "no sir", no matter the age of the Caucasian. This is a lasting vestige of a time when they had to fear for their lives when getting in the crosshairs of a racist and emboldened white person. Imagine the children being generationally raised in homes like that, what they heard for years and years about the things they needed to do to avoid getting Emmett Till'ed, and tell me that privilege doesn't exist. Even when society was separated by race, all other factors being equal, the simple fact of separation conferred privilege out of a hierarchical societal structure. This is exemplified in the 1954 Supreme Court case *Brown V. Board of Education of Topeka*:

Segregation of white and colored children in public schools has a detrimental effect upon the colored children. The impact is greater when it has the sanction of the law; for the policy of separating the races is usually interpreted as denoting the inferiority of the Negro group. A sense of inferiority affects the motivation of the child to learn. Segregation with the sanction of law, therefore, has a tendency to [retard] the educational and mental development of Negro children and to deprive them of some of the benefits they would receive in a racial[ly] integrated school system.

That was 1954. Not all that long ago. We know that peoples with ancient roots don't change their modes of thinking with swiftness and capriciousness. Americans tend to change quickly because we are a nation built partially on pragmatic actions in response to the incentive to get ahead. But blacks weren't an equal part of this country until almost two hundred years into its constitutionally organized history, nor was there any getting ahead when they weren't recognized to have equal protection under the law or the inalienable rights endowed by their Creator. And when Civil Rights were conferred, Democrats swooshed in with welfare and all of the negative after-effects I covered with the dexterity of Zorro with words that came before these words higher up in this Word document but to the left in the book you are currently reading. What's more, we are fifty-four years removed from the signing of the historic Civil Rights bill. Keep that number in mind. Sorry to tantalize you, but the answer is coming up right after this word from our sponsors.

Africans were slave traders. Yup. As if that lessens the evil nature of slavery. Don't qualify, equivocate, or rationalize it. Mind-numbingly obvious tautology alert: Evil is evil is evil is evil. I can't and won't fall in line with progressive commentators who say that white people are the worst people on the planet. I don't believe this because no one race, creed, religion, gender, or other societal grouping is running a monopoly on evil, nor righteousness. Nor is any one race, creed, color, gender or other societal grouping innocent on all points. However, reasonable people agree that owning another human being is evil.

Moving on. Sports and pop culture are heavily influenced by blacks. True to some point. But those aren't every day careers. They are out of the norm. We need to make black people in everyday careers the norm. Notice I didn't say "jobs" because a career is a high-paying job which you choose once you've attained the necessary education and training. A job is something you work until you can choose your career. "But Nate, black people are lawyers, college students, doctors, police chiefs, politicians, etc". True, but outside of a few exceptions, they aren't those things in major black centers. They have to leave urban centers to do so. The overwhelming majority of black kids in urban centers see blacks working dead-end jobs for life. Black communities are dominated by liquor stores, dollar stores, and fast food chains. Not the types of businesses or colleges that give young black kids hope of something better. Businesses that enrich lives, provide necessary services, give wholesome and family-oriented chances for entertainment, teach people new skills, and such are dying off in urban centers.

White folk often say "my race isn't as important to me as being black is to them". Okay, but since you see white people dominating all walks of life, why would race be important to you? Black people yes, have to make good choices and make their lives go a certain way, but by very dint of their skin color being at least a factor, they are more aware of their race and it's more important. This is where Republicans don't do a good job of seeing multiple perspectives. Just from engaging in personal and professional relationships, interaction, and casual conversation with blacks, I know that historically oppressed people don't dole out trust all that willingly. Folks who are used to suffering tend not to give the benefit of the doubt willy-dash-nilly. Republicans have put a lot of words out into the ether about how blacks should vote republican because democratic policies and actions are detrimental their community. This may be true, but just saying it won't do anything. A people that are distrusting due to history can't be convinced with words. They need to be shown, and the beginning of that process will be tenuous at best. But it's what is best, as reasonable people know that the give-a-man-a-fish paradigm and empty promises of the Democrats don't help in the long run.

We had a black president. That's true. I don't really have a great response to this one other than that accomplishment was a long, hard, road. And he was charming, eloquent, witty, funny, dignified, and had some good intentions. I disagreed with him on the role of government in ordering people's lives, but I disagree with many republican politicians on the same issue. If he spoke non-standard English, would there be any chance he'd have been elected? I doubt it. Being a teacher, I have seen many examples of the racism of low expectations. Whenever a white person points out how well a black person speaks, they are engaging in it. Chris Rock has a great routine on this from the late 90's regarding Colin Powell. I'd suggest you look it up and then get back to reading my book. I'm an English teacher and while I do spend much of my day silently correcting grammar, I don't equate lack of grammar skills with lack of intelligence. Lord spare me from my own haughtiness if I ever hold such a heinous belief. Much of white America does though and would never vote an Ebonics speaking official into the office of the president. To be fair, they'd probably never vote a grammar-hungry redneck into office either. Sorry Caucasians. I know what snitches get. I'll get the gauze out of my medicine cabinet in preparation for the stitches.

When I was a young man, my conservative sensibilities were offended by the term "African-American". Anyone who's read this far knows I've turned around on that practice. A label defining and identifying your racial demographic doesn't matter to me, and I support you if it's important to you, so long as it's honest and factual. Conservatives still grumble about this appellation, saying we Americans should define ourselves as Americans. I would agree if being an American wasn't so far down the list for me. I'm first and foremost a Christian. When I was a husband, that came second. Father came third. Being forced into divorce, father came second. Next is teacher, then Baptist, then entrepreneur. My denomination is not important as being a Christian because being a Christian is what takes one to heaven, not the sub grouping with doctrinal distinctives. Father, teacher, and entrepreneur are more important to me than being an American because I can love others, impact, and even change lives in those roles much more easily and profoundly than being an American. Were America to collapse and expire, I'd not stop being a father and Christian. I might even be able to be a teacher and businessman, so long as civilized society held on. So to me, it's not all that important if someone wants to hyphenate their national identity. It's not a sacred cow to me. This is a small thing to be turned around on. When one sees that small things are negotiable, one can engage in the inner dialogue that sometimes leads to different stances on the larger things.

And dear reader, reparations is an issue I've even turned around on. When I was eighteen I despised the thought of reparations. As a young man/old teenager, I distinctly remember watching a black pastor on CNN talking about how slavery was, in the long run, a good thing, because it brought his people to the best country that had ever existed. I am sorry I can't remember the name or the date of that interview, but you don't have to look far to find prominent conservative and Republican black voices nowadays arguing something similar. Redistributing wealth in the name of social justice is a communist ideal, and anti-capitalistic. I'm a capitalist. I believe in working hard and using what you earn to your benefit. What I'm proposing below is not a redistribution. But before I get to that, how about a little vamping? No? Too bad. It's my book. Nyah Nana Nyah Nyah.

Several years ago, I heard from a black coworker at my school district about a "Generational Curse" that is plaguing young black kids, especially boys. She is a person I admire, respect, and fellowship with on a regular basis. But I dismissed her idea as more jargon in the victim Olympics. Upon further reflection, I realized that there probably is a generational curse. Young kids of color are growing up in a desperate state of mind, and many of them make bad life choices. Propagandized hatred of your own face, while not as common and pronounced now, is a hard habit to kick. Here is where your friendly neighborhood conservative interrupts and screams "But what about keeping the law, making good choices, and personal accountability!" and that is when you say "Would you have turned out so well if you had to grow up in certain extreme conditions?" and then you and he proceed to argue for an hour or so. I know that just a few wrong turns here and there in my life and I would have ended up in an unenviable state. I think the curse is real though. I've already addressed the collective effect on the psyche of African Americans so I won't beat a dead horse. That's got a lot to do with the lack of collective success in this country. But I think the curse is a self-fulfilling prophecy also. Think about it. From the age of learning words to the age of figuring oneself out as a person, many kids are told, internalize, and come to believe things like "White people don't have your best interests in mind", "We will never get ahead", "This is not our country", "America is not for us", "Rap, play basketball, find a scam, steal, sell drugs, or fail", and other damaging ideas. By the time you were twelve, fourteen, eighteen years of age, would you not have internalized that despair, and make choices in line with it? So, if the curse isn't real, it's made real just by young kids believing it's real.

White privilege. Boy oh boy, say this in mixed company and you're in for a headache. Enough has been said about power structures, systemic racism, cultural trends, and wealth distribution that I can't really cover new ground there. I am looking at a few different angles below.

Ben Shapiro and his ilk state that you can't use racism as an excuse for the failures in your own life. This is true in a country of opportunity like America.

Liberals love to shout racism. Conservatives love to ignore it. By now, you possibly have noticed that I take a middle of the road position when it comes to human arguments and structures. I don't think racism is as influential in an individual's life as liberals make it out to be, nor is it as non-existent and irrelevant as conservatives make it out. I, like Shapiro believe you shouldn't blame racism for every setback and failure. Maybe you just stink at life. But I think it's at least reasonable to say that white privilege exists in some contexts. Maybe it's not as ubiquitous and all-encompassing as the social justice warriors say, but I think it does exist. I think affirmative action (a liberal idea and program) has actually contributed to it. Black people have to abide being considered "token" at their place of employment due to affirmative action. And when companies and colleges have to fill a quota, the unreasonable person who refuses to get to know their non-white coworkers can presume they do just that, not based on merit, and conveniently stop at the quota. Two good arguments for abolishing it, but that's a subject for another book. Just like the generational curse, I think the idea that it exists actually creates it. Look at the black community's relationship to police. It's a common thought that as a black person in an interaction with police, one has to be more careful than whites. Whether or not the statistics bear this out is immaterial. You believe something is more likely to happen, you are stressed out by it, you are more likely to be tense and on your guard, and you act accordingly. This stressed decision making leads to strained interactions, which leads to strained relationships. By the hammer of Thor, I wish that logic was still taught in schools. Logic as an academic discipline shows the natural progression of actions and consequences.

One need look no further than national restaurant chains to find privilege. Most of them, when their menu says "spicy" actually mean "spicy to white people". Except for Buffalo Wild Wings. As a whiteboy who is the exception to the rule of terrified white flight from spicy food, I have to give them much love and respect. Slow down crackers, and hear me out. If you think that adding Kelloggs Cornflakes; quite possibly the world's blandest and most boring food, to Mac N Cheese; a food already lacking in flavor, is "shaking things up" or "trying something new and exciting," you need to swipe right and plan a date with Seasoned Salt (it's okay to start with baby steps) and her even funner cousins from the spice aisle.

Beyond the less important realm of spicy food, there's the matter of slavery and segregation. Ultra conservatives are blue in the face screaming about how there's equal opportunity now. I don't wholly disagree. I just think the starting point was different. If you've ever played golf, you know the women's tee is several yards in front of the men's tee. We accept that women tend to be smaller and weaker in general and allow them to swing a little closer to the hole as an equalizing factor. Black folks have always swung from the tee farther away. Besides, it's hypocritical to say "never forget" of national tragedies like 9/11 and Pearl Harbor while simultaneously telling blacks to "fuhget aboud it" when it comes to the national, and much more prolonged tragedy of slavery. Slaves were freed in 1863. Okay, and then what? Did they stick around the plantations, working and getting along with their former masters? Of course not. They had to leave. Wouldn't you? Many came north seeking opportunity. To this day in Michigan, the majority of black folk speak with at least a hint of southern twang in their voice. This is not the white Michigan accent, which is quite nasal, rushed, and forceful with its vowels. Ask a white Michigan mom to say "pack the flash drive inside the backpack" and you'll see what I mean when she hits the A's. Black Michigan accents come as a vestige of the antebellum migration north. So there's leaving your home and migrating hundreds of miles without a job or means to survive. Did the plantation owners give a severance package? A golden parachute? No. The freed slaves had nothing to call their own minus the clothes on their back. Meanwhile, the land base of what constitutes contiguous America greatly increased with territory acquisition. The government was handing much of that land away to white natives and white immigrants. No restitution to slaves. No recompense for their suffering. No land to settle, cultivate, and use to make a profit. Meanwhile,

European-Americans had land, property, and wealth to cement their lives and those of their posterity in this country. Property is the precursor to land and land is the precursor to wealth. That's why it's so important to the development of civilization and society. Blacks had none of this.

Republicans love to tout the fact that Martin Luther King Junior was a Republican. What they conveniently ignore is that he believed that blacks faced much harsher obstacles than whites (the logical conclusion of which being that they deserved reparations once they were freed and given civil rights). In an interview (May 8, 1967) less famous than his Dream speech, he puts into words much more eloquently than I ever could (and in a more pleasing voice) the idea that you can ask blacks to lift themselves up by their bootstraps, but it's a ridiculous thing when most of them were left bootless. Later in this book, I make the argument that private property is what makes everything related to economics happen. Blacks had no property in general. The closest many of them got was sharecropping; a practice that was only partially just and which hearkened back the serfdoms of the Old World. When they wanted businesses, parks, schools, and colleges, they had to settle for black-only institutions. So when whites complain that there are black-only societal groupings, they must at least acknowledge this is a lingering effect of government and white society enforced black-only groupings. Being seen as

129

less than a full person went on for a hundred years. If you don't like the phrase "white privilege" because it sounds like modern jargon that is relatively new, at least admit the damage that was done.

In addition, they had no flag. Ask an Asian person living here what race they are, they probably won't say "Asian". That is a continent with many diverse peoples. They will say what country they come from. Even within that country there might be different ethnic groupings. When they identify as such, they are identifying with thousands of years of history, cultural markings, and traditions. There is a flag to march under in this instance. Hispanics as a group only exist in America (Richard Rodriguez's "'Blaxicans' and Other Reinvented Americans" speaks wonderfully on this matter), not the "Spanish" countries. When a person identifies as Spanish, they are typically identifying with a people descended from the Latins who, after pushing the Moors out of Spain, conquered and settled much of the New World's southern hemisphere as powerful mariners. There is history and tradition there, (along with much suffering, cough cough, people who believe whites are running a monopoly on evil, cough cough). Once again, a flag. With history and tradition comes guidance. Guidance in who you are and how you should present and conduct yourself. The same goes for many Caucasian people in this melting pot. They can trace their history to some part of Europe. If they say they only care about being an American, ask them if they had a stable home with stable values and stable finances and a stable and consistent morality practiced. If yes, politely ask them to look past that as their starting point when engaging in this debate. Ask many black people what race they are, and they will sadly, say "black", not understanding that a skin color does not an ethnicity make. Ask them what their cultural history is, they will say "Africa", not knowing due to Diaspora, what region, tribe, and flag their forebears marched under. They only have a vague idea of who they are and where they come from. This is made worse by the fact that many tribal regions in Africa had only oral traditions passed down, similar to Native Americans. Oral histories don't survive long when people's' lives are upheaval-ed.

By all the tea in China, the term "Africa" comes from a Roman emperor naming the Roman territories in northeast Africa after himself. So even the common term itself for the continent comes from western culture. It's why many folks have started to refer to Africa as "Amexum", one of the original, and self-applied names for the continent. I know this name hasn't really caught on, for as I wrote this paragraph in Google Docs, "Africa" was recognized as a valid word, while "Amexum" was not and had those squiggly red lines under it which are almost as offensive to the eyes as seeing WWII cartoons portraying Japanese people with squinty eyes and bucked teeth.

Look at your favorite literature and movie art.

What's the common ingredient in the best stories? It's a character who asks themselves "Who am I?" and through conflict and a compelling story, eventually come to answer that question. Han Solo did it in a positive way when he flew out of the sun to save Luke Skywalker from Darth Vader's gunsights. Frodo answered it in a negative way when he donned the evil ring whilst standing above the only thing that could destroy it. And so have many other characters from lesser artistic properties. Many white people often, in white circles, complain about black people not having social graces. I won't go any farther down that road as it could easily land in stereotype territory, and while stereotypes are never 100% true, they are 100% offensive. However, I would ask "would you have social graces if you and those who came before you didn't know who you are and where you came from?" In addition, black communities are overrun by crime on one side and harassment on the other. If survival attained only by constant paranoia was your primary goal for each and every day of your existence, would you possibly be lacking in the social skills society demands? And since many can't really get ahead, that small but insidious contingent of whites who want to keep blacks down (not acknowledging that a people can flourish without another falling behind) don't really have much work to do. Crime, poverty, government dependence, and pulling each other down are doing it just fine. Surely goodness and mercy, I wish logic was taught in schools.

A flag is a symbol, something to take joy in, an ideal to strive towards. African-Americans came unwillingly with no flag and still have no flag. Many Caucasians get mad when they see the American flag being burned or desecrated, or they get up in arms when others when folks don't want the Confederate flag displayed. Why get mad? It's just a piece of dyed fabric! We all know the answer. It's a symbol. It carries emotional (either positive or negative) and therefore, intrinsic value. My beloved friends with a melanin suntan have no such privilege that comes with having a flag to admire and march under. I'd see no problem with doing so. If someone is raising a family here, loving their spouse, working hard, abiding by the law, paying their taxes, and being a decent human being, I don't get all huffy if they march under a foreign flag.

I remember walking the Spanish section of Queens, New York, taking in the sights, sounds, smells, and atmosphere. I don't like NYC living because I prefer elbow room and my city shutting down at night. I don't say that last sentence to be flippant. New York appeals to many, obviously. Each to his own, and I don't begrudge anyone who does enjoy living there and is put off by my preferences. They are already contributing to America in those ways and means I just mentioned. I say let them connect to their ancestry without bothersome opinions constantly being thrown into the ether. America has continually put up real numbers when it comes to folks defecting from countries with less peace, justice, love, and prosperity. Just by coming here these folks have tacitly given America a wonderful complement. Making them march under the American flag during parades celebrating their heritage is wanting to have your cake and control the symbolic and constitutionally guaranteed free speech of it too.

I made my way to NYC for the first time in 2015 when a friend of mine was in a low point of her life and facing homelesseness. I went there to pick up her five-year-old-son and travel back to Flint, Michigan with him. I went through a bitter custody battle for my kids and could empathize with her as I didn't know until the battle was over what the result was going to be. Any parent knows it's a hard thing to face the idea of giving up your child to someone else. I ended up fostering him from May until December of that year when she got back on her feet. She's from Honduras originally and came here looking for a better life, which she found after some struggles. She's now got a fabulous job in the military and is more gung-ho about America than I am. She believes Spanish people should assimilate by learning to speak English. I happen to disagree, even though I walked those streets in Queens not being able to converse in Spanish myself. Were I to desire to have purchased fruit, vegetables, treats, trinkets, clothes, and a myriad of other items, I could have done so without the language barrier presenting an insurmountable obstacle. And I would have been engaging in trade with people who are selling products honestly. Demanding they speak English and think a certain way about every aspect and symbol of this country is just gross.

Conservatives love to point at the economic success of Asians in America, primarily those of Chinese, Japanese, and Indian descent. They say that Asians statistically do better than Caucasians. This reduces the idea of privilege to merely economic variables. It's too complex for that one item to disprove the whole argument. Caucasians drive the culture. Asians tend to stay in the cut. There are a lot of things beyond economic gain you can find more easily done when you are in the driver's seat.

Conservatives also defeat their own argument along the way. Conservatives take pride in their ability to debate. This is why liberals are so much smarter than conservatives. Now we all know straight from the mouths of loving and tolerant liberals in our lives that only racist, uneducated, and poor white people elected Trump; no one else. See what they do there? Rhetorical rigor plays second fiddle to identity politics, so they don't have to engage the argument, only their weakly contrived experiential validity of the speaker (failing experiental, immutable genetic qualities); rules determining said validity they conveniently make up and arbitrarily alter before the matter even comes to debate. A debater's (sometimes even a master debater's) ethnic origin, religious faith, skin color, genitalia, body type, number of hours clocked being buillied, special combination of fluid gender identity, and direction aforementioned genitalia points either contribute or entirely abolish a speaker's argument before it's even passed their lips. Easy-peesy-string-cheesy. By relegating themselves to the realm of reality and debates that at least pay lip service to making sure Lincoln and Douglas never hit the spin cycle in their graves, conservatives make a fatal blunder, one which is ever and increasingly becoming even more fatal-er. But, since they so ignorantly and blindly demand on real debate, they at least should level the playing field a touch.

How so? Well, by being consistent, of course. Conservatives have argued (rightly so) that big government, Democrat, and socialist policies are devastating to the families and lives of blacks in America. They then are stupid enough to throw in denial of institutionalized and state-sanctioned racism. Being someone with his eyes and ears to the ground, I absolutely see a vested Democrat interest in keeping black folks down (insert silenced pistol suddenly going off behind my head and a burly, scowling man straightening his suitcoat and beating a stealthy retreat after he gently lowers my head to the keyboard so as to keep my children from hearing the thud from their bedrooms). Instead of showing blacks how the Republican way of thinking, and maybe a few Republican government programs thrown in for extra oomph can help, Republicans shout at black people how they shouldn't be so monolithic in their thinking and dependent on government. Black folks, for the most part, aren't having that, needing to be shown instead of shouted down. Then, conservatives turn around and passionately deny white privilege. Can't have it both ways and call yourself rhetorically and intellectually honest, you silly geese. If government under the direction of a certain people of a certain political bent are destroying certain people of a certain melanin-rich bent, then we have white privilege being squeezed out the star-shaped Playdough Fun Station hole on the other side. Conservatives also argue that major urban centers—the places where black Americans are overwhelmingly concentrated—have been decimated by Democrat control and still deny white privilege. Dr. Reality should immediately issue a prescription for Getwiththeprogramillin and maybe a small dose of Stophamstringingyourownargumentalix.

Only more perplexing to me is that people of a certain left-leaning bent who argue that America and its government have enacted and continue to impose suffering on its people, and yet they want to continue handing over more and more power to order our lives to said government. Talk about self-defeating arguments. Seriously, talk about it. From my point of view that's a topic for another book, essay, vlog, diary entry, or rambling and incoherent Twit...Twut...Twert? I'll get it eventually. FYI, I'm not sure I'll ever write on that topic. I might not have any more writing in the tank after this instant classic, know what I'm sezzlin'? I intend to be the Orson Welles of political commentary books, weight problem and all.

Let's make this section even more uncomfortable. Those decrying white privilege are actually contributing to it. Squirming yet? Give it time and keep reading. Those who fail to concretely define it are adding to it. Above I state that it's not just about economic situations. Too often though, it's applied to arguments police brutality, political clout, lingering white racial hatred, or a vague yet all-encompassing conspiracy to keep blacks down. I think that if a concrete, definable, measurable definition and solution were to be generally agreed upon, work can be done to counteract it. Otherwise, you're demanding people change their hearts without evidence and using it as a catchall. Might as well punch at the wind to change its direction.

Beyond the words comprising this paragraph, I prefer to define LGBTQ people as "people". I don't see a person's sexual desires and activities as their most important traits. I love them and see them as fellow image-bearers of a loving and just Creator. But I must break from how I label them for the sake of this argument.

In my next example designed to make you uncomfortable, the LGBTQ community is adding to it.

Observant people understand that the claim of white privilege and the vast majority of LGBTQ come from the left. Here's where the connection is clear to someone willing to dig a little deeper. The "T" is a hotly debated issue right now. Enough has been said about the ethics of everything going on but not much has been said about the privilege of the thing. Dave Chappelle said it best. The T smacks of white privilege. Black men are identifying as women and engaging in social interactions which draw public attention, but this whole subject is given credence because there are more white men in this society, and by logical averages, there are more white men identifying as women and engaging in social interactions which draw public attention. The widespread acceptance of young men going to the ladies' restroom, changing in the ladies' locker room, competing, winning, and setting records with women in track-and-field events, and even literally beating women into bloody submission in the MMA arena is due to white men and their overall ability to drive culture, social constructs, and politics. Conservative white men like to say that minority and special interest groups have political clout because of their professional victimhood. When you add white men to that equation it becomes less controversial.

Once again, Dave Chappelle is a prime example of that. There was immediate backlash from his first Netflix special when he dared to make jokes on the subject of transgender men. So much so, that he addressed it in his third special, and made up a story about dancing at a club and engaging in sexual activity with a transgender man, along with the aforementioned quote about this smacking of white privilege, saying that if black men were the only ones doing this, society would tell them to be quiet because nobody cares what they think. It's a joke, yes, and not entirely true, but also not entirely untrue. Black men are the most marginalized group in America. They have less political, economic, societal, and other forms of power than any other group. Black men, more than any other group, have been pushed to the fringes of society by their government, business, law enforcement, white Americans of means and power, and many black mothers to boot. When it's possible for a black man to "victimize" a transgender man, you know the victim hierarchy (which conservatives and reasonably minded liberals understand does exist) has been jumbled. As of 2019, his fifth special is causing even more consternation because he refuses to stop making jokes about the transgender community. By constantly playing the victim against a black man who is doing no more than making a living telling jokes, they are setting themselves in importance above a group of people infinitely more aggrieved by America's history than they. And please don't talk to me about comedy fueling bullying, hatred, and violence. People committing/inclined to commit such acts would do it without the inferred egging on of a comedy routine.

Not to mention, comedy is a tool for normalization and acceptance. Criticism is a tool for differentiation and rejection.

Uncomfortable yet? No? Take a breath, because here comes the deep water. Black people are adding to white privilege. Take a minute to glance around nervously and get over the knee jerk guilt you're feeling after reading that last sentence. I'll wait. Done? Here we go. I've seen it in action in my own life. As I've stated above, I'm a teacher and a landscaper. I've seen white privilege in action in both components of my professional life. Dismiss my experiences as anecdotal if you will but I believe they stem from a deeper problem.

As a small businessman, I spent the entirety of 2017 and the early parts of 2018 with a black partner. In the name of fairness, Johnny and I agreed that we wouldn't fully combine our businesses. We would split 50/50 any jobs we brokered and worked together. This was because I brought a little more to the table in terms of clients, equipment, and investment capital. He brought a little more to the table in terms of tree-dropping skills and word-of-mouth credence. So we were both free to acquire clients and do jobs on the side without throwing the wages earned into the pile. It worked out, and he and I were able to be a blessing to each other. When it came to jobs worked together, that's where the equal split was supposed to happen.

Here's where the white privilege came into play.

Johnny refused to work jobs alone which I brokered and scheduled in white neighborhoods. I've always had a mixture of white and black clients, but he would only go to my black clients without me. Even a couple of my black clients didn't like him because he's loud and boisterous (Johnny, you're learning this for the first time as you read my book, so I'm sorry in advance). He believed that he would be seen as suspicious working in white neighborhoods alone. I've already talked about perception guiding action so I won't get into whether or not this was true. I have worked for hundreds of people and I would be a fool to believe that all of them were upstanding people free of prejudice. However, I've got no qualms about working in areas where I'm the only white guy, and so on several occasions I finished jobs without his presence and collected payment and forwarded his share to him later. I never had any problems due to my race. In my experience a white person is much safer in a black neighborhood because the fear of police retaliation if a white person were victimized is real and tangible. Once again, we are in the area of perception guiding action. What's more, there were a couple jobs Johnny brokered without me but asked me to help due to my more capable equipment situation. It's no secret black people like supporting black businesses. That practice is applicable here. Johnny abjectly refused to collect money from my customers. However, on more than one occasion, one of his customers handed me money with Johnny standing right there. The white-face-in-charge concept is real and sadly applicable here. This goes back to the generational curse mentioned earlier in this book. Black folks were taught to hate their appearance and race by evil whites in the past. This has a lingering effect. "Just get over it" is too easy of an apothegm. Long held beliefs and feelings are dreadfully difficult to drop.

Now, my teaching experience. I worked in a predominantly black school in a predominantly black city. Makes logical sense that the student population would reflect the community, even in a charter school where parents have to make the conscious choice to send their kids there. Even more so, the school was dominated by persons of color in leadership positions. As a quick side note, I can't give up all my conservative roots and would argue that in certain work situations like this, government jobs, leniency given by Child Protective Services, and giving out of government benefits, there is such a thing as black privilege, but that is such a small percentage of society and it's in response to whites controlling much of the power here that I can't fully fault African-Americans for engaging in it. Maybe that language is too strong. I'll say I understand it. It's possible to understand something without justifying it. We as humans default to comfort and the path of least resistance. Anyway, I probably wouldn't ever be the superintendent of this school. If I was, it would take years for me to endear myself to the community at large in order to accomplish that. I did what I could and for the most part, was given tremendous support by the parents I served. If race was part of that, it only proves the idea of white privilege. I saw my fellow black teachers and administrators excoriated and attacked (both verbally and physically on a couple occasions) by black parents. Not once did I see anything of the sort, even from parents who occasionally disagreed with me on ideas and behaviors.

I believe it had a lot to do with the way I carried myself when interacting with my students. I try (sometimes fail) to be loving, inviting, attentive, and caring. It's amazing how many teachers are horribly weak on these virtues. No foolin', in my travels I've actually heard teachers utter the words "I hate kids". That's akin to a composer hating those weird marks he makes on lined paper, a carpenter hating wood, the ol' oak tree at the ol' swimming hole next to the ol' mine hating summer breezes, a cobbler hating shoes and peaches, an engineer hating pocket protectors, George Lucas hating obscene overreliance on CGI, a fireman hating fire, a freedom fighter hating his ability to fight freedom, and a social media influencer hating…whatever it is they work with.

I wasn't terribly good on modern jargon of teaching, analyzing data, and doing some of the things that are drudgery for teachers. I maintained a standard of academic excellence in my classroom and was still accepting if one failed to achieve it. My students who maintain failing grades and goof off are still human beings, and I still showed love to them. Parents appreciate that. Frankly, I think it also had something to do with race. I am not the best teacher in the world, and probably wasn't even the best at that school. I didn't go out of my way to give tutoring to those who were apathetic to academic achievement. For my own peace of mind, I would help those who actually cared. The goofballs didn't care, and I have a personal policy of not spoon feeding my content to the goofballs. They are not babies, nor would I treat them as such. I would try to mentor them in terms of bigger life lessons, and that made me a bad teacher in some folks' eyes (primarily my bosses). To me, if a young man doesn't know how to conjugate a verb, but does know how to carry himself like a gentleman when interacting with a female; I don't see myself as a failure. I came to have a reputation in that school to the point that students started referring to me as the "white father" or "cracker dad" of the school. I really don't mean to brag. This is a part of my experience that I will always bear and cherish, no matter how smug I might be coming across just now. These were terms of endearment, and bestowed despite the fact that there were older, more experienced men working as teachers there. Word spread to the community and I was given much love and respect by the mothers whose kids had adopted me as their father figure. One hardly ever recognized quality of black folks is that their grapevine is much more alive and vibrant than that of white folks. That, combined with the fact that black people in black communities are sick of white people coming in and leaving when a cushy job comes along, or not serving their community altogether, led to my being given favored status. Race is not the most important factor in our lives, but it does play a role.

Here's where my privilege really shined. I am an English teacher. We are a dime a dozen. This is shown in the disparity of English teacher wages compared to math and science teacher wages. I worked in that school from 2012-2018's school year end. I left once in the middle of the year for a job that wasn't much easier, but I was horribly frustrated by the direction the leadership was taking it. Year end, the superintendent and CFO backed the money truck up to bring me back. The following was a good year due to the leadership making changes that took us in the right direction. The next year that leadership was fired and replaced, and I was once again horribly frustrated by those positive changes being reversed in lieu of getting student numbers (re: funding) up. I found and accepted a position in a different school. My employer came and offered me more money and a chance to leave the classroom for an easier job in the district. My 9th grade students went quite a while until a replacement was found and were served by a long-term substitute in the interim. That's on me, to some extent.

I was going crazy though and wanted to love my job but didn't at the time. Here's the kicker. Conventional wisdom says that when you've accepted a job somewhere else, you don't accept a counteroffer because you paint a target on your back as a drama queen who needs to be replaced with all expediency. I accepted the counteroffer because I loved the students there, not the leadership, of which I made no secret. That should have painted an even larger target on my back. I should have been seen as an agitator who refused to toe the company line. I wasn't. The next year (2017-2018 school year), they had fired another English teacher and needed someone in the 11th grade classroom. Once again, the superintendent (a new one; that place had a revolving door of CEO's when I was there) backed up the money truck and hired me to come back to the classroom. During this school year, I didn't do everything the way leadership wanted, and even called the MIOSHA office on the school because the students were coming to class on the second floor in unacceptable temperatures because the heating system wasn't maintained and fixed properly. Repeated calls to my principal and the building administrator didn't fix the problem, but a call to OSHA did. By August 2018, my lawn business expanded to the point that I could sustain my bills from those wages and I had started working on my master's degree. So I resigned. I figured I wasn't all that welcome anyway. Point is, I actually was an agitator that didn't toe the company line.

Compare that with the experience of my close friend, Russell Andrews-El. He came to that school the year after I did, so we had comparable seniority. He is of Moorish descent (he refuses to call himself black), and a Muslim. I'm a Christian. He taught Math. A non-white, Muslim, male Math teacher in a predominantly black, Christian community is like seeing Bigfoot riding a unicorn and a leprechaun following behind with Chupacabra on a leash. You may not know, but it's a byword in the teaching community. When you find a black male math teacher, you hold on to him. I lived an hour from work, so I left the minute we were contractually allowed to be with my kids and run my business. Russell stayed after on a regular basis to tutor in his content, despite not being paid to. I only coached soccer one year I was there. Over multiple years, Russell built a competitive robotics program from nothing by recruiting kids and building corporate partnerships. That was a commitment of four days a week after school (while he was also tutoring) and at least one Saturday a month from September to February. My soccer season only ran from September to early November. Russell offered to work on his prep hour when a teacher shortage in the middle school necessitated high school teachers taking on middle school students. I guarded my prep hour like it was one of my children. I was offered raises to stay there. When Russell offered to work on his prep, he proposed a temporary raise based on the extra hour each day he would be working. Temporary, mind you. They refused and made no counter-offer when he, out of frustration, found a job closer to home in a safer, less chaotic, and higher achieving school that was located on a college campus (i.e. an easier job). I was an agitator, and Russell was a banner-bearer. All things being equal, I gave them every reason to get rid of me, he to retain him. What is this but white privilege in motion? I can't help myself. I have to make this uncomfortable again. Black people were the leadership of this school. Black people are adding to the concept. Once we sit down and have some uncomfortable conversations on this, we can all stop yelling at each other and solve it.

Got ants in your pants yet? Here's another way blacks are adding to white privilege. They scold each other on a stereotypical basis. Scroll down Facebook long enough and you'll find memes, pithy quotes, and all-out rants citing various types of evidence as to why blacks need to do better on a corporate level. Click on the comment section and you'll see some blacks saying "amen" and some saying "but this" and some saying "white people also" and some saying "you're proving the point" and some saying "I'm an exception and take offense" and some saying "only American blacks" and some just engaging in argument with each other. All but the most brazen and indecent whites leave these comment sections untouched by their two cents, but whites definitely do observe this kind of stuff. Occasionally social media posts go viral that are critical of white culture, but it's usually along the lines of humor, like our proclivity to have boring names or shy away from seasoned food. It's not direct and firm criticism of culture disease (yes, I know it is sometimes when a racist white person does something stupid/wicked/worth attention). Problem is, black culture in America is too widespread and too diverse to engage in blanket school-marming. Blacks who do this add to pasty, melanin-deficient privilege.

Then, ask yourself, is it easier to be a white celebrity, or a black celebrity? White celebrities, outside of rare moments, have it easier than black celebrities. Black people are making it harder on black celebrities (uncomfortable yet?). White celebrities aren't pressured constantly to "give back to their communities". Do white celebrities not come from communities? Do they just spring out of the ground, ready to dance and sing? Of course not. They just don't get asked to financially prop up others in a collective sense. Are white celebrities asked to be role models on a scale like black celebrities are? Doesn't appear to me to be the case. Are white celebrities father figures to young white men and teaching them to be men through their movies, songs, and music videos? Not at all. Yes, white celebrities, when they step out of their lane and say something political or provocative, are given the business by social media and Fox News, but that doesn't put being a white celebrity on par with being a black one. There are white celebrities who support Donald Trump. Do they get as much hate as Kanye West got when he paid a visit to 1600 Pennsylvania Ave? Remember what I said about black people adding to white privilege (<u>feel free to start squirming in discomfort...</u>)? Here's another example. A black celebrity can't leave the Democrat reservation and think for themselves without being called a race traitor, Uncle Tom, coon, or house nigger (<u>.... now.</u>). Remove this type of monolithic thinking along with the infighting over skin tone among the culture, and African-Americans can stop adding to white privilege. I feel like I've said "black", "African-Americans", "whites", "caucasians", and "white privilege" a lot in this book, no? There's not a racial thesaurus website, so far as I know.

People on the right get obnoxious when they demand celebrities do their job and not be political. People on the left get obnoxious when they demand their celebrities walk in lockstep with the Democratic Party. Both positions are cynical and don't give credit to celebrities for being intelligent, free-thinking, and thoughtful people. Everyday people who aren't politicians engage in political discourse at their work, in their blogs, and on social media. No one tells them to just do their job and shut up. It's condescending, rude, and doesn't recognize that person as an equal. At one point I was only qualified (in the job market sense of the word) to work a minimum wage job, e.g. my teenage years. I decided to work a job walking and picking up the leavings of kenneled dogs. I loved that job more than any other job I've had, besides teaching. I've not spent a day of my life not being owned by a dog and I am happier for it. In addition, that place employed a bunch of interesting, friendly, and gorgeous women, and I was friends to all of them. I had a crush on a couple but was a pudgy dork lacking in confidence and horrifically intimidated by them at the same time. Even then, nobody presumed to silence my freedom of political, religious, and symbolic speech. The things coming out of my teenage mouth would have been even more lacking in intelligence than the political, religious, and (weakly) symbolic speech you've absorbed, maybe endured, as you read this book. Think of how dumb I came across then and thank your stars I didn't write a book while I was learning to drive and crushing it at Super Mario Brothers.

One more example and then I'll be done, promise. Think of the way people converse when it comes to suicide and substance abuse. White people (specifically men) are more likely than blacks to commit suicide. White people are also more likely than blacks to engage in opioid and meth addiction. Much talk about mental health help, recovery, compassion, sympathy, and other positive emotions and actions is being thrown about in response. The fact that many people who engage in substance abuse end up horribly hurting their loved ones and those in their lives, along with creating many criminal issues including property theft and death (meth lab explosions happen often enough to make jokes about it without having to explain the impetus for your joke) is often ignored in lieu of the compassion these "diseased" people need. Blacks are more likely to engage in crack addiction and alcoholism. Both of these also lead to crime and early death. Where is the same compassion? Do blacks have to go and just figure it out on their own? Does the high rate of death of blacks in conjunction with the crack epidemic not matter, as it's not typically a suicide issue? As a conservative, I see the legal side of this and would like crime and dealing drugs to stop and those engaged in criminal behavior to be incarcerated and reformed, but as a compassionate person, I see that help and sympathy is needed for all people who fall prey to substance abuse, not just those from the dominate slice of society. You fill in the blanks as this being another example of:

_ _ i t e _r i v _l e _e. Don't let the poor little stick figure die from hanging folks.

Mark this down as a historic moment; a white conservative arguing for the concept of white privilege. As I've said before, will say again, and am about to say now, I see a perfectly reasonable middle ground in all non-theological debates. You can't dismiss the other guy's argument out of hand just because he's on the other side. One can entertain a thought and peck at it like a hungry chicken without wholly ingesting and synthesizing it. Conservatives can entertain the idea that privilege exists without conceding that it's all-encompassing and deterministic to the lives of non-whites. Liberals can entertain the idea that non-whites are adding to it without conceding that there isn't such a thing. Both can recognize and agree it isn't as pervasive, ubiquitous, and oppressive as some portray it to be. I believe, like Candace Owens and Ben Shapiro, that you can't blame white privilege on your lack of success in this country of opportunity. However, I also believe, like BLM and much of the Democratic party, that there is such a thing, and that it accounts for extra hurdles (sometimes put up by the very sermonizers on white privilege) black people face. You might notice a trend in this book; the idea of middle ground where both sides can be appeased instead of constantly throwing barbs at each other. I intend to ride this and many other fences all the way to the bank (maniacal laugh). I do believe in absolutes in the realm of morality and the supernatural. Beyond that, it's hard to cement absolutes in the realms and structures we humans set up for ourselves, partially because those things we erect and so feverishly fight for are often tainted in the matter of integrity because they come with an agenda.

Moving on, I'm neither Republican nor Democrat. However, if I was to run for president it would probably be as Republican, because of my own moral leanings and our ridiculous two-party only system.

I would also run as Republican because Democrats have always been anti-black. Whether during slavery, segregation, or the welfare era, they and their ideals have always damaged black lives, which, I think we've established, matter. Southern Democrats upheld slavery. The KKK sprang out of this demographic. They murdered and terrorized southern blacks. Dixiecrats fought tooth and nail to keep segregation and inequality alive. Margaret Sanger wanted abortion rights so as to keep undesirables (re: non-whites) out of the breeding pool. Welfare programs maintain a laser focus aim at poor blacks. Blacks were and continue to be targeted for the "benefits" of welfare, and the after-effects of welfare are damaging to the black family, and by extension, American society as a whole. What makes welfare evil on par with slavery and segregation but subtly different is that the latter two are not at all dishonest. They are up front and open. Welfare cloaks its damaging effects and agenda in the name of benevolence. The cool thing about welfare for those insidious Democrats who want to be seen as the generous benefactor is that they keep their system in place, unchanged, and continue to be voted into office by people of all colors who want the welfare system maintained as is. Now, non-blacks can sign up for a form of oppression that is not up front and honest about what it really is. When you allow a powerful, faceless entity to dictate your life and actions to you in return for a paltry subsistence, it's an updated form of slavery. It's only by the miraculous grace of God that some blacks have, as conservatives are fond of pointing out, risen above these circumstances to attain wealth, land, power, and influence.

Now, an appeal to the Bible. Many conservatives are either Christians or amenable to the Biblical economy of morality. If you're a liberal atheist, this section isn't for you. Take comfort in the fact that I'm making an appeal to conservatives to make a change. It's been fifty-four years since Lyndon Johnson put pen to paper, and (allegedly) made a terribly offensive remark about black people voting democrat from here on out. Fifty-four years are a little more than two generations. Why is this important? Exodus 20: 5 states:

"You shall not bow down to them or serve them, for I the Lord your God am a jealous God, visiting the iniquity of the fathers on the children to the third and the fourth generation of those who hate me."

The third and fourth generation of those who hate me. This passage, as can be seen in the first part of the verse, is addressing the idea of following other gods and what will happen to the posterity of those who do. Doesn't apply in this discussion? Well, I would ask you if the Bible is an efficient book. Systematic? Not really. It's not laid out in a chronological or systematic manner. Multiple books often recount the same stories or elucidate the same doctrine. The most systematic book is Romans because the Apostle Paul knew that the Romans had a system for everything. Other than that, it's not systematic. It is efficient, however. If you believe in a creator God, you believe that He had knowledge of every transgression that will ever be committed, and could address multiple transgressions with one group of words. And our forefathers who owned slaves were hating God by enslaving and withholding the rights of blacks.

If a human has a soul, imprinted on them in the image of God, then hating them, or treating them in a hateful way, oppressing them, and murdering them are all hating God. It's not just the same ballpark, it's not just comparing similar things. It *is* hating God. I John 4:20 is perfectly clear about that. No way around it. What's more, the verse is addressing the first and greatest commandment, the one that commands only worship of God. By owning another human, or denying that other human full humanhood, you are setting yourself above them, thereby worshipping a being (yourself) other than God. Either way, you're toast, along with your progeny. God is visiting upon the descendants of those who hated blacks the sins of the fathers. It's no wonder SJW's, progressives, reparation apologists, black supremacists, and people who see no moral wrong in persecuting whites are running full tilt (or maybe just getting revved up) right now. We are in the beginning of the third generation for this Biblical warning. I don't even think it will stop with the fourth. By saying the third and fourth generations, God was leaving open the idea that it could be ongoing. We need to fix the effects of this injustice. While I'm not responsible for the sins of my forebears, and blacks today cannot claim victimhood to the level of yesteryear, I believe that it's possible, righteous even, to be part of the rectifying of these sins, especially were it to change the statuses and hearts in future generations of our historically poorest and most downtrodden citizens.

In addition, the American Indian had a rough go due to Andrew Jackson and other like-minded monsters. Native Americans are so small in population and so weak politically that we mostly keep them out of sight, out of mind. As if that makes it any better. So what I suggest below for African Americans should also be prescribed to Native Americans, along with being granted their own land and not reservations occupied at the behest of government. I'm Native American in descent, but I have providentially been spared reservation living. I thank God for it. Living on land that the government won't wholly cede to you is depressing, and doesn't encourage investing in, working, and cultivating said land. Were the government to enact my plan below for Native Americans, I'd refuse the benefits. I'm by no means rich and have suffered much discomfiture, but I've done all right, and this book is my early retirement plan. If we all do our part in buying, reading, and giving copies of this book out to friends and family at Christmas time, any grave injustice I've suffered at the hands of my ex wife, smackheads and thugs who have stolen from me, and the decisions of my younger, dumber self will magically be made all right by the dune buggy/amphibious assault vehicle I intend to buy and use to amphibiously assault a fortified stronghold housing some ponytailed, chronically scowling types with the profits.

So tell me what we do, already. You're droning on and on. We can't institute forty-acres-and-a-mule. It's unfeasible because every inch of land in this fair country is owned privately, commercially, by sovereign Indian tribes (or occupied by less than sovereign tribes), or by the government. If you try to start taking away land you'll have civil unrest at the very least, civil war at the most. That's not even scare tactics or a slippery slope argument. Folks won't have anyone taking their land. I'm not saying it's right but it is reality. I am compassionate to the stolen land argument but can't see an easy way to rectifying that historical injustice without bloodshed. So, as I've posed earlier in this loquacious tome, money is a fabulous motivator.

I think I've devised a way that will not make either side of the aisle terribly mad. Maybe even some will be moderately pleased with it. That's all I can ask for at this point. Step one. Get up, shower, shave, and have a morning coffee or line of potent cocaine. Your choice. There's a lot of work to be done. Step two. Institute a program which awards any descendant of oppressed people of legal working age twice the amount of their most financially lucrative fiscal year as reparations from the government. Give them a reasonable number of years in which to take advantage of this program. Basically, motivate them to get it done as quickly as possible. Step three. Figure out a year to cut this off. There must be an endpoint (something government is really bad at figuring out). The children still in their formative years have time left in which to see their lives better and learn to make productive choices. The children who are twelve, thirteen, and fourteen have already had much damage done, so they should be able to take advantage of the program once they enter adulthood. Step four. Give tax incentives (or extra votes, as I suggested earlier, above, recently, and in the past) to corporations, companies, private individuals of means (particularly black individuals who don't need this program but would like to be a benefactor), and trade incentives to other countries who donate specifically to this program, making it possible even to designate to whom their money goes so as to increase human interaction and brotherly love. For blacks who choose not to give but also want to opt out, there must be an incentive like temporary but significant reduction of income tax or increasing of personal voting power. Step five. Encourage African Americans who have not reached their earning potential on previous tax returns to head out in December and get second jobs and work like mad men, accumulating as much taxable income as possible in the coming year so as to maximize their future payment. Watch the tax revenues roll in, the unemployment rate bottom out, and welfare dependency among the poorest blacks noticeably drop. Step six. Have financial specialists in place when it comes time to hand over the money. These are people who can work with individuals to make a plan to turn this money into more money. This involves personal living budgets, savings accounts, retirement plans, stock portfolios, business investments/startups/latch-ons, land acquisition, and life insurance. We don't have an aristocracy in America, but it is true that many folks come from what one could label "old money". Business investments, stocks, and life insurance plans will ensure future generations of blacks will come from old money. Step seven. Watch the country once again strive and move towards American exceptionalism, this time sans the inequality that still existed in the fifties and sixties (the golden age of the American worker and middle class but not so much an age of racial equality). Not within the next eight-year reign of whoever holds the highest office, but definitely within the next couple generations. Step eight. Tear down the white guilt bank (not immediately but eventually) and stop arguing about the existence of white privilege because there is no need anymore.

You like that? I even did it without help from my dad. Revolutions start with revolutionary ideas. Liberals can be happy that reparations are happening. Conservatives can be happy that it's not through redistribution of wealth, and is predicated on hard work and capitalist ideals. Also, it's not a cookie-cutter approach. Not everyone gets the same thing. Everyone gets what they earned. Seems to me that's a good working example of fairness. Any dogmatic Republicans whose faces turn cherry-red at even the mention of white privilege and reparations could at least take solace in the fact that if reparations were enacted by a republican legislature and sitting republican president, there would be a massive voting shift back to republican for black Americans. Most blacks actually live their lives with conservative ideals, are at the very least amenable to Christianity, believe the money they make should be kept, enjoy baseball and apple pie just like the next guy, and (except for a few large cities like New York) don't engage in abortion at a higher rate than the other races. The problem with conservatives is they are going no further right now than saying "Democrats are bad for black people". Historically oppressed people don't bet their trust money on another horse with just a few words and criticism of large, Democrat-controlled cities. They want to be shown a plan. Responding with "just work hard and make your own life better" isn't a plan. If conservatives think black people wrongfully count on the government to better their lives, give them a plan where the government can help them be better through government programs that incentivize exceptionalism over a meager paycheck and food stamps. I think we'd see a mass exodus of blacks from the DNC if this, or some variation on it happens. If a utilitarian view of the matter won't placate them, I have nothing else to offer. Conservatives are free to exercise their freedom to inveigh against me in the forms of blogs, books, and rambling Facebook posts often and passionately. I would ask that they just be cool and not call me fat. I'm pretty sensitive about my weight.

Litigation

THERE ARE TWO types of people in this world. The first type is the type of person who says "there are two types of people in this world" to serve the point or agenda they are vomiting from their cigarette hole at that moment. The second type is the type of person who realizes that humanity is far too diverse to categorize in a binary fashion and roll their eyes when someone in a movie or television show (see below for an example) says "there are two types of people in this world". But, in the realm of litigation I'd say there are two types, at least when we are in that arena. There are people who are looking, waiting, lurking for the chance to be victimized and those who understand that life is complex and often couched in suffering.

A quick but memorable line from *Pulp Fiction* says that an Elvis Man would love a place like Jack Rabbit Slims. This is attached to a deleted scene in which Uma Thurman's character says to John Travolta's "There's only two kinds of people in the world: Beatles people, and Elvis people". Now I'd love to think that I'm an Elvis man. I mean, come on, right? Elvis was so much cooler than the Beatles. He was the bad boy but not too bad. Women wanted him and men…know what? This section is already suffering from trite quotes. He dressed cool, he sang cool, he had cool hair, and he danced cool. In his movies he acted…that's another story. Elvis was the man.

Me? I'm kind of a dork. Not only did I get straight A's in school, but those A's came quite easily. I got either a 28 or 29 on my ACT. It was one of those and I'm so far beyond the point where it even matters. I would read entire novels in a weekend. I followed the rules. I corrected my friends and coworkers when they broke the rules. I was truly sorry when I got in trouble and showed real remorse for letting down my parents and authority figures. I respected authority. *The Lord of the Rings* is my favorite book and movie. I have outgrown video games but at one time thought it a real accomplishment to finish Metroid or Super Mario Bros. I was good at sports but jealous of those with leaner bodies and better athletic skills. I've always struggled with weight and food. I kick myself when I get caught up in a black Google hole of fan theories for *Star Wars* and Marvel Comics movies but I read them nonetheless. When *The Office* came out I was instantly hooked, wishing I could be as cool and laid back as Jim but realizing I was more straight-laced, intense, and excitable like Dwight, except for his obvious autism. I love football but having gone to a small private school, I was never given the chance to play it organizationally. I throw a really good spiral but never had more success at it beyond pickup games. I was and am to some extent a nerd. I was and am a Beatles man. I've been bullied many times for my nerdiness. I didn't suffer from prolonged depression from it, nor did I shoot up a school, but it definitely affected me negatively.

Beyond being bullied, I've suffered in a myriad of ways. I've had my money and landscaping tools stolen by terrible people whom I've called friends and invited into my house. I've had a car totaled by a person driving without insurance and on a suspended license. I've been assured the money they owe me is being sought after by a collection agency but I'm not holding my breath. I've been ganged up on and beaten down. I've fallen twenty feet out of a tree stand that a friend who was horribly qualified at even the roughest form of carpentry built and erected. I worked in a place where coworkers said such vulgar, profane, and provocative things about me, my (then) wife, and daughter I puke a little in my mouth to recall to memory. I've been called all manner of things and had my life threatened by people holding a gun or a knife up to me, when all I had was my wits. I had a child one year to the day out of high school and struggled ever since. I have been caught up in moments where I was being so ugly to my fellow man I didn't think I'd ever be able to take back the words I've said or repair the damage done. I hurt my back at age twenty-two due to property upkeep negligence of my landlord and suffered chronic pain more days than not since that incident. In grade school I got in trouble when the actual perpetrator of an injustice put lies on my name. I've lost jobs unjustly. I've lost a twin brother to cancer. I've discovered a girlfriend was cheating on me through text messages. I've lost another girl-friend because I have custody of my children and my paramour wished me to be a weekend dad. I've lost a wife to adultery and divorce. I wouldn't wish the mental anguish adultery invited into my life on any person, be they just or unjust. In April 2019 I signed a loan to acquire a hotdog cart. I turned the money over to a professional fabricating shop who assured me it would be ready by early June and I could have several months left of warm weather to make money off it. Come August, it still wasn't ready because the parts they ordered from China were tied up in Customs due to Trump's posturing and threats of tariffs. I col-lected the cart when warm weather had fled and must wait until spring/summer 2020 to start profiting from this investment. I've felt the sting of my choices and the choices of others quite intensely. I've not suffered more than many and I have suffered more than some.

And yet through it all, I never sued anyone. By today's metric, I could sue my ex wife for the emo-tional suffering her adulterous choices imposed on me. I didn't sue the landlord whose leaky drainpipe over the porch led to the sheer coat of ice I slipped on and consequently hurt my back (if it had been recorded, I'm sure my fall would have been comical from an outsider's or viewer of AFV perspective). This was contrary to the lawyer I consulted who said it was a slam-dunk case. I didn't sue the junkie who stole my $1,000 Stihl chainsaw earlier this year. That's more out of my living with reality. I don't have a good address for him (he moves back and forth between multiple places) and don't feel he would show to court or repay my money anyway. He's been arrested more than once so I'm sure having another blemish on his name doesn't much occupy his thoughts at night. As a side note, protect with your life your Stihl tools, fellow handymen. When smackheads and no-good-nicks see the Stihl orange, Stihl is what they want to do (that's a play on words). I didn't sue the doctor who told us my twin was going to make a full recovery. I didn't sue the parents of the many children who have bullied my two autistic children just for being different. I didn't sue Trump for his playing the tough guy with China. I lost possible income over it, but I don't begrudge the man his choice even though I don't support it. He had reasons which he thought were good. I've moved on and kept my heart free of bitterness against him. Besides, some of his other choices have led to more suffering for others.

A reason I don't identify with either major party is that they spend their years outside of the presidency telling the American populace that the guy in the Whitehouse is going to spell the doom of our country (see the fear mongering I discuss in the introduction). Please. Our country is too strong, too unique, too strong-willed, has too many checks and balances, too many people on the lookout for corruption and chicanery, and too many guns for one man to destroy it in its current form. When Trump is either voted out of office in 2020 or term-limited out in 2024, I kind of wish the people who have filled my Facebook feed and editorial segments on cable news networks with doom-and-gloom about how he's worse than Hitler, going to take over and become dictator-for-life, or blow us all up in nuclear war to eat a very specific amount of crow. Maybe we can spend the next calendar year kicking them in the shins free of consequences or something.

Another reason I don't identify with the major political parties is they are teaching the American people to be victims and always at odds. People are looking for a reason to be victimized by someone else nowadays because when you can convince a third party with a modicum of power that you've been victimized, you are just a hop, skip, and a jump away from convincing them to force the victimizer to recompense you. It also feels good to be at odds with others. For some reason I can't explain it fuels our pride to pose oneself in defiance of another person/persons we deem to be in transgression of some avenue of morality, rather than pitying, praying for, or trying to help them. It's why so many people who have scrapped many elements of traditional morality hate racism so much. It's incredibly easy to not be a racist and to look down on, criticize, and scold those who either are, or are labeled as racists. Politicians who engage in fear mongering, hypercriticism, and doomsday punditry are posing themselves in opposition and just trying to keep their party's interests in the fore and power in their hands, or trying to get it back. I don't know if that equals what's best for America but I have a sneaking suspicion...

Anyway, many folks don't share the same view of suing that I do. I have been sued. I was sued by a client over a business deal that went south. I was sued for divorce by the aforementioned ex. I had to pay my lawyer fees, her lawyer fees, and spousal support; Michigan's form of alimony, for the first fifteen months. She sued to force me to become a weekend dad and sued for more than half of my income. She lost (that's a story for another book). Years later she was in the valley of life. She asked me to employ her with my business. She then stole tools from me and pawned them for drugs, by her own admission. In court, she and I agreed that I would pay half of the cost for her drug tests so she could prove she's clean and enjoy her parenting weekends. Six months later I discovered that she was filling out and printing a fake drug test online, and pocketing the $40/month I was giving her. I filed a small claims case against her for this money and the tools. Then the day of the hearing I didn't even show up. I have an intense, visceral reaction to all court proceedings and didn't care to follow through with my case. Years later she got her life together and was making a meager wage at her retail job. In early 2019, the Friend of the Court pulled us in for a hearing to determine what back child support she owed me and what she would pay going forward. Despite all that she's done to and taken from me, I have done my best (and failed on many an occasion) to release my heart from bitterness and resentment for her. Also, I have built a profitable business and have many more professional options than her due to my college degrees, skills, and experience. I told the FOC I didn't need or want support from her, as I wanted her to continue getting her life on track without a reason to be bitter at me (garnishment of wages being a strong reason to do so). That didn't sit right with the Michigan Disbursement Unit and they determined they were going to take from her wages in spite of what I said. I believe the government wants money changing hands because it's money they know they can borrow against if the need or desire arises. So for two months in early fall of 2019, I received $500 from her wages. And then the money stopped. I didn't get a notice in the mail, a phone call with a new determination, or anything. I reacted by letting this new development roll off my shoulder and moving on with my life. In the middle of January 2020 I learned that they had started putting that money in a bank account and the card they were supposed to send was lost in the mail. It's only investigation on my part which led to this and the restoration of that child support. But it's not like it broke me. I washed my hands of that money in February 2019 and only begrudgingly accepted it later on when the government decided I was too stupid to make decisions for myself.

I don't think that all lawsuits are wrong, sinful, or unjust but I'm very wary against using this as a device to disseminate monies. John Stossel puts it nicely in his book *Give Me a Break*. Lawyers are like missiles. We should keep a few around just in case we need them but not go crazy manufacturing them. I don't get litigious for four primary reasons.

First, I'm a Christian. Paul's letter to the Corinthians commands them not t be litigious with each other. Many Christians take that as meaning "don't sue other Christians". My answer to that is this. If I forgive and refuse to sue someone who is on their way to heaven, why would I sue someone who might not be on their way to heaven, to whom forgiveness over a wrongdoing—be it egregious or petty—is altogether foreign to them and on whose heart I might have a positive spiritual effect were I to forgive them?

Second, lawyers aren't value-added. In the current form my professional life has taken, I'm a business owner in one hand and management in the other.

Being a business owner, I've come to the point where I can employ someone else to do the hard labor. In fact, this year is the first of my eight in business that I only did catch-up labor when equipment breakdown or rain hampered my employee's daily lawn schedule. The last lawn I mowed was in the first week of September. Giving the hard labor to someone else and collecting the profit is the goal of starting your own business. Being a manager, I have the choice to delegate physical labor to my subordinates. I happen to enjoy labor very much and I pitch in when sitting at my desk just isn't doing it for me. I told my current employer I would be a bad employee if my job entailed sitting at a desk all day. I don't say this to brag. Rather, that's to my shame. It's a shortcoming on my part. My attention span isn't what it once was, and my body says it's time to sleep when I'm sitting down for a prolonged period of time. So, I get up, go outside, oversee, supervise, communicate with my subordinates, and chip in when the fit takes me or when they need the extra help. As a business owner and as a manager, I'm not value-added. My work of delegating and decision-making isn't tied directly to making money. The hourly employee in between my decisions and the product/service is the one adding the value. Apply that to civil suit lawyers and you'll see what I mean. They don't make money by providing a necessary product or service. They take money from one person's hand and put it in the hands of another person. Yes, they do often have a client who has been legitimately or deliberately hurt by the first person. I will concede that point. But it truly is a zero-sum game. The money that changes hands isn't creating more wealth for all. It just changes its address. The loss of it makes the original owner's job at replacing it more difficult. As a capitalist I am not totally at ease with that. I want money to change hands in fair trade. As a Christian, I am also wary of money ill-gotten. God doesn't bless wealth of this nature.

Third, quantifying suffering in terms of dollars and cents is just so random to me, and also makes me feel kind of gross. I believe we all bear the image of God, making everyone's life equally invaluable, no matter the monetary, skill, height, lifespan, or physical beauty differences between us in this life. To say my life or someone else who suffered or died was worth X is so arbitrary and weird. And determining X is often in the hands of people who don't really appreciate the sacred nature of being one of God's image bearers. Earlier in this book, I do contradict myself a little bit and lay out a plan for slavery reparations (pump the breaks and take a beat, conservatives, I have a spiritual reason to do so) but that's because of the sheer amount of death, unrecompensed suffering, and devastating after-effects this country's institution of slavery imposed on a people.

Last, I am a Christian. Have I mentioned that once, twice, thrice, or eighty-frice in this book? I have an easy answer to suffering. It's caused by sin. Sin is caused by man. Ergo, suffering is caused by man. The devil is the author of sin. He wished to be as God and was thrown out of heaven. He used the serpent to lie to Adam and Eve about eating the fruit, compelled them to sin, thereby cursing the world. This world, although it is wonderful and beautiful, groans under this curse. It is only a shadow of what it was before sin entered the world, and just a weak, corrupted hint of the sinless world to come. Call me a foolish religious person parroting fairy tales if you must, but I have an answer to suffering. It's always happened and will always happen so long as sin abounds in this world. God does not cause it, but He does allow it. Can I divine the will of God as to why suffering takes on certain forms, or why some in this life feel the curse of sin more acutely than others? I'd be a fool to try. What I do know is that suffering teaches us much more wisdom than pleasure.

As a man who has had desperate, misguided people steal from him, I've been able to become more vigilant and guarded with my things, protecting them and my ability to make a living with them more diligently. I also am an extreme extrovert. I love people and love being loved by people. I am naïve and trusting, often giving the benefit of the doubt despite the evidence pointing out how foolish this is. One time the aforementioned Johnny Brown pointed out to me that he observed a Spiders tattoo on a man we interviewed to work with us. I was ignorant of the Spiders but Johnny told me they are a local white supremacist gang. This man, perfectly pleasant to me and Johnny in the interview, might have had ulterior and sinister motives in store for us (and specifically him) had we hired him. These experiences have shown me to stop befriending and trusting everyone I meet. Furthermore, I was raised with a hoarder's mentality that's been difficult to kick. Losing things to theft and the natural wear and tear effect work has on them, I've been able to let them go more easily and keep sight of the fact that things are just things, nothing more. As a man who lost a twin to cancer, I've been able to compassionate and empathize with people suffering from cancer, along with their loved ones more profoundly than I could before. Through my twin brother's life and even at his funeral, many people came to the saving knowledge of Christ as their personal savior. I doubt he'd give up his short time of suffering in exchange for the everlasting souls saved through these events. As a man who was brought so very low, indeed nearly to suicide, by adultery and divorce, I've become more able to rely on the help of others and God, not on my own feeble strength, in times of difficulty. More importantly, I've been able to minister to men and women suffering the same or similar circumstances. Would I trade my own suffering and those chances for ministry for a happy and ongoing marriage? I really don't think so because I know I would have learned nothing by now and wouldn't have met and been able to help others in these life circumstances. I also would have never been a teacher. God has made Himself so real to me on many occasions. I was always happy having a wife but not in love with the jobs I worked while married. She filed for divorce. I begged and pleaded with her to be forgiven and reconciled to me even when I found out about the adultery. She was not content to do so. The ensuing depression left me to forget about taking care of the work at the place I was employed. This coincided with that company faltering financially due their ongoing and expensive litigation with a former partner company (I'd say there is a lesson here that helps prove my thesis of this chapter right were I a wiser man). So they started downsizing and I was one of the first to go, being depressed and less productive than my erstwhile married self. Being downsized at that job led to substitute teaching, which led to teaching, which led to the happiest I've ever been in my professional life. What is that but God giving me joy even in unhappy times?

Through all this, I have concluded that it's neither government's job to stop all suffering, nor to repay it. Suffering is common to mankind and the natural course of life. Most of the time, we humans can move beyond, learn from it, keep on living (indeed thriving) in spite of it. I wasn't guaranteed an easy life when I was born, nor has it been easy. But it has been productive, fruitful, and full of joy. Asking a government that has caused suffering to fix suffering is like gifting fangs to a snake and entreating it not to bite.

We have a huge problem with a multitude of lawsuits in this country. They are their own out of control corner of the system, have a cottage industry devoted to their proliferation, and end up costing everyone money in a host of ways. Here's what government does need to do.

Set a limit on what a person can be repaid for. Not all physical suffering is equal. Smarter people than I can determine the level that deserves to be eased with money, but I'd say anything < a broken bone is a good place to start. Bumps, bruises, scrapes, stitches, and injuries of this nature aren't out of the ordinary. Actually, most of the people I know have broken a bone in their life. I've never done that (thump on lumber) and don't intend to so I drink plenty of milk and ingest the occasional head of broccoli. Point is, a broken bone happens often enough to call it common. Short of it happening while being pinned to a restaurant table because the guy seated a few feet away from you was wildly enraged by you and your existence and decided to do an elbow drop on your shoulder, I wouldn't say suing is the best kneejerk on the docket.

Not all emotional suffering is equal. People literally have sued others over name-calling and neighborhood dogs barking. I don't like to throw around the S-word, but that's just silly. I have suffered emotionally on a level I can't put into words and I still don't feel like money would have made it any better, were I even be assured of receiving the money the court awards. The problem with humanity is that it is humanity and humanity is prideful, sinful, opportunistic, and cunning. When people know they can find a lawyer to sue others over petty things, they will. Were limits put in place, fewer lawsuits would happen, the system wouldn't get bogged down by frivolity, fewer taxpayer dollars would have to be pumped into it, and more people would learn to move on with their lives, reconciling their hearts to the fact they ate an Impossible Whopper prepared on the same grill as meat-filled Whoppers.

Set a limit on the amount of money a person can be paid. This is where I advocate for the fed to oversee, maybe even supersede the states. The amounts of money being tossed around in lawsuits is not standardized and is obscene in some cases. A simple Google search will reveal some of the more shocking stories out there. It's no secret the rich and rich companies get sued more than the middle and poor classes. When the rich go or are perceived to have gone astray, people are crouched at the ready to pounce and take their money. It's part of what drives the various forms of insurance up, which in turn drives the cost of their products and services up. Those who get rich from suing those entities with deep pockets and a wealth of resources don't have to feel the sting. They are now rich. Doctors and companies go ahead and pass the added costs onto their customers. It's a vicious, self-feeding cycle.

Force the losers of frivolous lawsuits to pay. Tort reform needs to happen, which means human reform needs to happen. When someone files a lawsuit over a frivolous reason and loses, they really don't lose, other than the time they put into it. Most civil lawyers don't take any pay unless their client wins. Here in Michigan we have generational lawyers who have made a living chasing ambulances and forcing doctors to perform cesarean deliveries despite the fact that birth defects and complications haven't been lowered by the ever-rising numbers of this procedure. Lawyers who take frivolous cases play the law of averages, knowing if they throw enough boogers against the wall, one of them is bound to stick at some point. When a person or company is being sued and they lose, they pay. When a person files a lawsuit and they lose, they should be forced to pay not only damages, defendant lawyer fees, but also court proceedings. I'd love it if people who sue over a minor afternoon headache are forced to cut a check to the defending lawyer, bailiff, and stenographer facilitating the proceedings. It's what the Swiss do. Guess what? The Swiss people have adapted and don't sue frivolously. They are also some of the most well-to-do people in the world. So there. Na-nana-boo-boo.

I can't even begin to describe the emotional liberation that happens when one refuses to be a victim, takes ownership of their suffering, rolls up their sleeves, works hard to overcome it, and dissipates all bitterness and resentment towards the person who caused it. I can't describe the emotional liberation because I've done all of these steps and have tried many times to describe the emotional uplift to others, always to no avail. This is including suffering brought on by my own choices. I've forced myself to love myself even when I'm unlovable because I'm a creation of God and an adopted child, and He won't abide me hating one of His own. Putting aside the religious aspects I've discussed for the sake of the irreligious among us, I guarantee with a 90 day money back kind of guarantee that this country would see an age of personal responsibility and determined spirit were government to disallow us from springing at the chance to be a victim.

I have spoken.

That pig-faced guy voiced by Nick Nolte in *The Mandalorian* is my favorite character from a canonical *Star Wars* show I really want to like but which at times is even more hokey and cheesy than that Wilford Brimley 1985 made-for-television Ewok movie.

Welp. That's an awfully weak way to end a chapter that got really deep and grimy at points. Turn tape over.

Insurance

ANY WAY YOU stack it, insurance is a racket. We need to hack it, smack it, and rack it after enjoying the comedy stylings of Buddy Hackett. 'Scuse me while I initiate a paragraph break before we all get caught up in the flow.

Rackets are supposed to be illegal. By most mainstream religious and secular worldviews, they would be defined as immoral due to the nature of using the money of others to drive one's own cutthroat agenda under the guise of offering "protection". Think about what you're paying for when you pay for insurance. You're paying for something to protect you from drastic life-altering consequences when disaster strikes. You're betting that you'll be okay when disaster strikes. The insurance companies are betting that disaster won't strike. They're taking your money and the money of countless others and investing it to become richer than rich, but not sharing that money with you. When disaster does strike, they do their best to make sure they pay you as minimally as possible (or not pay you at all, cough, cough, deductible, cough) so as to protect their precious money. And they have the law on their side. One cannot drive a car, own a house, run a business, or do any number of things without insurance. Now, insurance exists because many people cannot fundamentally be trusted and too many knuckleheads ruined a good situation for the honest folk in this world. This is not entirely the fault of the insurance companies; they've just capitalized on it.

In addition, you're basically paying for nothing. You're paying for a piece of paper, if you're like most people and never have to file an insurance claim. Even those people who have to file a few claims in their lives still shouldn't have to pump thousands of dollars a year into a metaphorical lottery machine and never see that money again. If you walked into a grocery store and handed a check over each month for $700, you'd expect some food and necessities back, not a promise to take care of you when famine strikes. If they didn't hand over what you wanted, you wouldn't sullenly shrug your shoulders, walk out, go home, and hope that you didn't get hungry. That's foolishness. I propose we do away with insurance, or at least insurance in its current form.

As I said before, enough untrustworthy souls took advantage of enough people so as to get the government involved. Too many hit-and-runs, too many unreturned phone calls, too many this, too many that.

So government made people get insurance in order to step into society and engage in various risky activities. That needs to change, and people need the option to engage in these things without having to pay exorbitant prices for them. I believe insurance is one of the things that keep working class folk poor, hence the common intersectional criticism of the system being rigged. I'll start with car insurance. Except for rent, and maybe food depending on the size of the family, car insurance is often the biggest monthly bill for the poor. Speeding tickets, accidents, taking out a loan and not actually owning a car, location-based increases for living in large high-crime cities, and other factors make insurance hard to afford for the poor, making a bad situation worse. I know because I've been in that situation.

We live in a technological age that will allow us to give people the option of not having insurance, but still having accountability if they mess up. I used to have a device on my car that tracked my driving habits and lowered my insurance rates for being a responsible driver. Why can't the government issue similar devices to car owners who don't want to pay for insurance, and know they will be responsible if disaster strikes? This can be a tracking device that either is hidden from the owner, or connected to the on-board computer and which shuts the car down in case of an accident, the car being stolen, or the driver engaging in criminal activity. The person would know their driving was being tracked from work to other places and home, and they would have to be fine with that in trade for not having to pay for insurance. This would encourage them to be extra careful drivers, put their cell phone on airplane mode while driving, respect and obey the traffic laws, all while allowing them to save the money they might otherwise be spending on insurance for the future in order to buy a better car, luxurious insurance, or any number of things that could help them better their life station, even be it vintage beanie babies.

It will also cut down on theft of vehicles in big cities. Unless thieves become expertly skilled at shutting down the government-installed tracking device, they will be at the mercy of police soon after stealing the car. This will in turn drive down insurance costs in large cities, thus allowing people who live in these cities to possibly get out from under government oversight and afford better insurance, thus giving them the chance at bettering their future prospects. Like I propose for the health industry at some other part of this book you'll either read later or have already read (I'm kind of tired as I write this sentence, too tired, in fact to finish the), a cheaper government option should also be proposed. One that doesn't have the extravagant coverage of a private company, but would suffice in a pinch. Michigan used to have this. It was called the Uninsured Driver's Fund. It existed in the 1970's. My dad took advantage of it as a young engineering student. He would pay $75 in January and was covered for the year by the fund, thereby able to save money during his college years. The Michigan Uninsured Driver's Fund is now defunct and Michigan is a no-fault state with high rates of vehicular theft, reckless driving, and the concomitant high insurance rates. With the tiny difference of $75 being much less nowadays, we could institute such a government program with reasonable rates and protection for the poorest among us which still holds them accountable if they show themselves to be irresponsible or opportunistic while on this program.

Similar things can be done for home, boat, business, and other types of insurance. If a person wants me to remove a tree from their lawn, and said tree is hanging over their house, they know they incur a certain amount of risk doing it themselves. Hence, most reasonable people won't hire a guy like me unless I'm insured and have a proven work record. These can be easily ascertained in the digital age through websites, Facebook, and phone calls. And they don't have to ultimately go with me as their guy. Freedom of association is an implicit right within the 1st Amendment.

Or, how about this. During George W. Bush's presidency, the idea of health savings accounts saw their advent. Skyrocketing health insurance costs brought this idea into existence. Before, one paid healthcare coverage through their employer or a private plan, and that was it. You lost that money. Even if you never went to the doctor, dentist, or emergency room, you lost that money. Voila, health savings accounts arrived. Now, you could pay into a plan, use that money to cover visits and prescriptions, and keep it if you didn't use it. Why can't we do this for other forms of insurance?

The insurance companies should be bending over backwards to come up with creative plans for you to pay into their service, allow them to take their operational and investment cut from your premium, and keep the rest in a health savings-esque account. Were I to have a couple hundred thousand dollars to start and operate an insurance company, 15% or some comparable figure of every insurance policy would go towards this account. This would be a way for me to set myself apart from the competition, despite not making as much profit as them. If you have car-related costs like repairs, tires, oil changes, cleanup, tickets, and accidents, you should be able to use this money for these costs. If you don't use the money in your account, it should accrue and eventually act like a savings account or certificate of deposit, where it exponentially grows in a year as a reward for not touching it and being a responsible driver/owner/operator. It can then become your deductible in the event of calamity. In real life, you're using your own money as a deductible anyway. My insurance company would allow you to use money you've already saved through our service as your deductible.

If not needed, you should also allow it to be invested and see a return if you so choose. The insurance companies are doing just that with your money. They're not just covering their operational costs and saving it. They invest it in the market and see exponential returns. That's how several hundred dollars during a calendar year can turn into half a million in life insurance when the person dies. Insurance companies, instead of competing with each other to make the most and have the most customers, they should be competing with each other to make their service as attractive, affordable, and rewarding as possible for their customers. A rising tide floats all ships.

Minor Political Parties

SPEAKING OF RACKETS, let's rap about our two-party system for a minute. Pardon me while I pull up a folding chair and sit backwards in it casually so as to put the young people at ease. Not since Teddy Roosevelt has a third party won the presidency. Third party wins in lesser political roles are also few and far between. I don't wish to contend the negative or positive of Roosevelt's tenure. I just respect his win tremendously. Disillusioned with the Republicans, he went and created his own party, engaged in a brilliant grass-roots campaign, won the highest office, did a pretty good job, left office, went to Africa to shoot some exotic game, and got his face on the side of a mountain. Mad props. Since then, the two major parties have made it part of their game to keep the little guys from even having a spot in the game. That's not American. A least in theory. In practice, holding your hand on the forehead of the little guy while he comedically swings at thin air might very well be extremely American.

Republicans partially blame Ross Perot for Clinton beating Bush senior. Democrats partially blame Ralph Nader for Bush junior beating Gore. Those third party guys, while not having a chance to win, did end up splitting the vote for the party they were somewhat aligned with in philosophy, but not in name. I say we should give these guys a seat at the table, if not for anything else, for entertainment value. The debates with Clinton, Perot, and Bush were fascinating and funny. Perot made it his business to make Bush look stupid. It was hilarious and gave Dana Carvey comedy fodder for the ages. If you're a child of the 90's, I guarantee you're saying "Can I finish?!" in a nasally voice and southern drawl in your head. Ever since then, the little guys have had to have their own debates (in a form of "well isn't that cute" condescension) while the two guys the major parties nominate have the real one. It's a shame because it's born out of fear. The major parties know that third parties split the vote, so they rig their debates, primaries, and state caucuses to keep these guys from even having a shot. I think it's the opposite of the democratic process. It also goes against early American practices, in which the man defeated in the presidential race would become the vice president or a member of the president's cabinet, so as to give the "other guys" a voice in the ear of power.

In the early stages of 2019, Democrats were writing open letters to Howard Schultz begging him not to run. Republicans might have a similar situation down the road with a third party candidate playing spoiler. What is the best reason the two major parties can marshal in defense of keeping a third party out of the race? Keep them from splitting the vote. That's it. No appeal to morality. No credible doomsday scenario where it spells disaster for our nation. They just want the vote split two ways to better ensure their chance of winning. Political parties who doggedly act in a manner to preserve the party and its interests have lost sight of what being public servants really means. If every party were given a legitimate chance in the race, the vote would be fairly split instead of a third guy taking votes from his ideological cousins every once in a while.

Think about it. Would we not benefit from new and fresh voices in the political arena? Would we not benefit from having a party more specifically aligned with our political beliefs for which we can, in good conscience, cast a vote, instead of choosing the "lesser of two evils"? Would we not be able to vote for a major party candidate in better conscience once we saw some of the lunatic fringe parties spouting their nonsense on a major platform? I'm looking at you, American Communist Party, and Alt-Right. Would legislators not be forced to engage in more across-the-aisle cooperation if there were representatives in Congress who couldn't be tied down to voting strictly down partisan party lines? Would there not be more accountability and less corruption if the good ol' boy network was weakened? I think all phases of government would benefit from some fresh ideas and faces. Just a thought. If we try this and it's a disaster, I'm going to throw a smoke bomb and beat as hasty a retreat as my dad bod allows.

Our country might even consider abolishing the party system, and letting candidates run on their own individual merits. Democrats are a fractured, dysfunctional, cannibalistic family, but they still know what's best for you and yours. Republicans have maintained a stranglehold on their ultra-conservative base despite stabbing them in the back and abandoning them when the going gets tough. Public perception for the two parties is a confusing and frustrating dance in which divergent styles get tangled up with each other. We could put an end to it all and let candidates stand on their own tiny platform. Twenty-four hour news coverage and instantaneous access to all the information humanity ever recorded allows the electorate to make informed decisions for candidates based on their political stances, voting and legislation records, and personal moral conduct and history. This would save candidates the embarrassment by proxy when prominent members of their party engage in chicanery and no-goodery. It would also abolish the idea of "protect the badge" mentality when said chicanery takes place and the party must hunker down, spin, spin, spin, deflect, deflect, deflect, and engage in what-about arguments. That, along with news outlets deciding to go back to the old ways of reporting what happened without journalistic bias, pompous analysis, and sensationalism (ratings be damned) will ensure a less corrupt and more purer form of democracy sees its day in court.

Police

TREAD LIGHTLY, NATE. Tread very lightly...................
(these dots represent time and train of thought)
..............................Nah. We clearly have a police
problem in this country, but it's not as everyone describes it.

Just like all industries populated by human beings,
there are some bad police in this country. Problem
is that when a police officer messes up, suffering often ensues. We have accountability measures, the
law, proper procedural rules, and other things to keep
them in line. When a cop steps out of the law, he or
she is supposed to be duly punished. Despite modern sentiments and perceptions, this is most often the
case. It's difficult to do a cookie-cutter approach because cops are humans, prone to mistakes, and a cop
who shows bad judgment and poor split-second decision making shouldn't be treated the same way as a
cop who willfully breaks the law for personal gain or
prejudiced reasons. I see the validity of both the Black

Lives Matter and Blue Lives Matter movements, and I wouldn't entirely align myself with either of them. This is because we are so polarized and galvanized in this society that simply saying "They have some good ideas" awakens the us vs. them cage-match to the death mentality too common among politicians and Facebook comment thread participants. Fun fact, both of those groups, along with Twitter warriors, were awarded the exact same grade for maturity on the Nate Roberts Scale for Group Maturity. You don't want to know what the grade was.

In 2017, a Black Lives Matter chapter leader down in Kentucky made a list of demands white people can do to eradicate racial inequality. Many of the points and requests she made were inflammatory, provocative, and downright offensive. You can look her treatise up online if you didn't hear about this. I couldn't fall in line with her ideas. But I understand where she's coming from. Enough seconds, minutes, days, months, and years of believing that this country isn't for you will take a person's psyche to a dark, paranoid, and disturbing place. On that same note, I watched *Flint Town*, a fabulous documentary on Netflix based on my hometown. One of the personal commentaries I saw in there involved two black mothers telling the police where they can find someone who's been terrorizing their neighborhood, and then chatting with each other about how the police want black people to keep killing each other so they won't have to deal with them. It seems like lunacy to an outsider's mind but to one who tries to understand the perspective, it's not so much lunacy as an extreme point of view born of despair.

Also in 2017, a black Wisconsin police chief by the name of David Clarke became a popular conservative commentator, criticizing Black Lives Matter and the violence that has taken place within the black community. Much of what he's said has been overly critical of black folk, inflammatory, and provocative. I couldn't fall in line with parts of his message. But I understand where he's coming from. Enough time spent seeing your brothers-in-arms suffering and people with your skin color making bad choices, and you too might become jaded and inflammatory.

Something needs to happen, and soon. Black and white liberals I know believe civil war based on race and socioeconomic boundary lines is coming. Black and white conservatives I know believe the same thing. God help us if this happens. In conversations I've had, many people are caught up in prognosticating who would win. This is horrifying. The situation of killing fellow countrymen over political and philosophical differences which could easily be solved can't really have a winner. Black and white fighting in the streets and countryside, rolling over those who refuse to join. It's a situation ripe for authoritarian takeover and martial law. God help us if this happens and the wrong man saves us from ourselves. Healing between the black community and the law needs to happen and both sides bear responsibility.

Chris Rock, in a recent special, said that police should be paid more, to a shocked reaction from the audience. For his punchline, he said "You get what you pay for" to enthusiastic applause. He's right. Police are underpaid. Think about it. When $35-$45 thousand a year is your promised wage, and you have to follow the law even when the law hampers progress, and you have to put your life on the line to do your job, and you have to keep the people you serve happy in extremely stressful circumstances, and you have to be hated by those whose lives and communities you protect, and you have to live with the constant threat of punishment and prosecution by those who oversee you if you step out of bounds for even an instant, the only incentive the government has left to appeal to in order to recruit police is the desire to "make a difference", "serve the community" and other higher ideals. Police who don't live with those lofty ideals become burned out at best, corrupt and incompetent at worst. Their wage is barely a living. Many police have to pick up jobs doing security, handyman work, and other things just to get by. Is it any wonder that some bad apples have seeped in and ruined the good name of the police? Money is a fantastic motivator. Police who do their job, maintain healthy relationships with the community, and walk their beat in a respectful and dignified manner should be rewarded financially on a regular basis. Police who don't do those things should either be punished financially or weeded out by the rescinding of financial reward, or other punitive measures. More money (and the seized property of those who profit from organized crime) should be allocated to policemen and women who do their job and do it well. There are all sorts of ways to raise accountability and accomplish this goal.

Since the police ask that people live and obey their authority when they are involved in a situation, I see it as their responsibility to begin the healing between the police and the black community. I practice the same concept as a teacher. I never break a relationship with a student unless that student steps out of line. I also never use my own problems and drama as a reason to snap at a student. As I write, this, I'm suffering from a sixth theft of my landscaping tools and various possessions from my house. Two of them were perpetrated by my ex wife. One of them by a guy I naively trusted and hired to come to my house and work on my landscaping tools. He was around my kids when I wasn't there and stole a chainsaw right under their nose. I don't go to school and snap at my kids because of this drama. I stuff my feelings in my pocket and keep it moving. Doing otherwise would be unprofessional, even though my students often use their problems as a reason to snap at me. When a student is disrespectful, I correct them in a firm but fair manner without a lovey-dovey way of packaging my words. However, when they've seen their error and aligned themselves back to respect, I tell them I love them, smile, crack a joke, and get them to smile again. Why do I repair the relationship when they are the one who broke it? Well, because I'm the adult and I'm in authority over them, and the secret truth about this situation is that since I can't use physical force and intimidation, I only have as much authority as they give me. They are much more likely to submit to my authority if they love and like me. With the factor of adult-to-child relationship taken out, the police's relationship with society is much the same. It's on them to repair a strained and often broken relationship. And yes, to weed out those police who engage in racist and unfair policing practices.

The black community must bear some responsibility here. The overwhelming majority of blacks are not criminals. However, statistics bear out that too many blacks are committing crimes against fellow blacks, their communities, folks of other colors, and society at large. I've already addressed prisons, reform of the legal system, and incentives for stopping the cycle of crime, so I won't beat that horse. Submission to authority must come, even when it is not enjoyed. Folks who are hypersensitive, here's the part where I won't tread all that lightly and will make you uncomfortable. I know from interaction, experience, professional/personal relationships, and friendships that African-Americans are a passionate people. This is a blessing and a curse. Situations in which healthy conflict/confrontation is needed can lead to positive solutions. White people, by contrast, often avoid conflict to keep an uneasy peace, but turn around to backstab and gossip about the person who disagrees with them. The flip side to black passion is due to their passion, some conflicts get way overblown and fall out of control. Stressful situations with police tend to bring out the wrong end of that passion. White folks are not guiltless when it comes to disrespectful interactions with the police either. Not by a longshot. And it's getting worse. Look up "Sovereign Citizens" on YouTube for a few weeks' worth of entertainment. My personal favorite is P. Barnes. He's my new hero. Seriously, look him up. It's even worth putting this book down for a moment to do it. Folks who willfully submit to authority in the event of interaction should be rewarded and not punished for that submission. Every situation is case-by-case, and personal recording devices on police and private citizens have allowed us to make determinations case-by-case.

In addition, the black community must learn to work with police. Trigger warning: This is where we must give up the unwritten no snitching rule. I cut lawns in the parts of Flint dominated by black folk. I cut lawns for elderly people and widows. I have several lawn customers who are old ladies living next door to gangbangers and drug dealers. They bar their doors and windows, look around to make sure the coast is clear before opening the door, and slip my money through a crack in the door, praying that no one finds out they are living there alone. They have lived there since the time that Flint was a thriving, bustling, and wealthy city. However, the no snitching policy in the black community has done nothing but make matters worse. What this does is allow the opportunistic, violent, and aggressive minority to take control and keep the content, peaceful, and passive majority living in fear. Black folk speak and act more collectively than any other community. They must collectively decide that enough is enough, and that their neighbors, nephews, nieces, husbands, wives, cousins, uncles, aunts, grandsons, and granddaughters who intimidate, beat, kill, rape, pillage, steal, and deal must not be tolerated anymore. Often, students who are "cool" with me accuse me of "snitching" when I write them up upon the occasion that they cross the line and do something that can't be shrugged off. First, I tell them that "no snitching" is something that goes between friends, and we aren't friends. I'm a teacher first. Second, "no snitching" should only be applied to things that aren't going to make others suffer. For example, you shouldn't snitch when your friend lets a cuss word slip. You should "snitch" when your friend steals a phone from someone else, whether that someone else is not a friend. Third and last, I tell them that it's not "snitching" when the peace is kept and enlarged. I've actually done a tangible good when I enlarge the peace. As a teacher I need to take actions to ensure those both happen. When others suffer due to "no snitching", the peace is broken and shrunken.

Then, the police can step in here and help by enlarging their forces. I advocated earlier in this book that America needs to stop allowing other countries who can't get their act together from leaning on our perpetual help. We also need to stop policing the world. Both of these actions will necessitate a reduction in our military, but not a drastic one. I believe that many of the skills regarding personal discipline, protection of the weak, and service to the country that are practiced by the military are similar to, if not even more developed in some cases, than those of the police. That's not even mentioning the large numbers of former military who step into police work. If we were to start bringing our military home and securing our borders, many of the men and women in service can be transferred to reservist status, and trained to be policemen and policewomen. This reduction in military activity will be an increase in police. Another point of the *Flint Town* documentary that stuck with me is that my city of 100,000 people is staffed by 80 police officers, a staggering ratio, and the worst in the nation. One of the lieutenants on the show laments that his officers are mostly in cruisers driving around and not walking the streets; a measure made necessary by understaffing. More police on the force will mean more police walking the streets, working to cultivate, develop, and maintain positive relationships with the community. Silly viral videos of cops dancing and playing basketball with urban youths will be an ancillary benefit. This will mean that communities will be safer while simultaneously repairing the tension that has existed for quite some time between the police and the black community. Will it be easy or immediate? Of course not. But it is necessary.

Corruption

HUMANS ARE HUMANS, and sin will always plague them. However, accountability and consequences, along with the occasional religious and moral stances will constrain them. It's no secret that government is corrupt. While we may have brilliant checks and balances to restrain this, it still happens through any number of loopholes and ingenious ways.

I deem it a vulgar thing that lobbying groups hold such political power. The elected officials in government are supposed to represent the people. Lobbying groups don't represent the people. They represent a hyperactive group of people with an aggressive agenda. Were I president, I would abolish all lobbying and lobbying groups. Officials should not be in the pockets of those who would further their status in this life, be they businesses, fringe crazies, or otherwise.

The Graco corporation should not use the law to enforce the type of car seat I put my toddler in. This, ladies and gentlemen, is the very definition of a conflict of interest. They should make the best car seat available, and leave the choice up to me. Lunatic fringe groups who believe in the eminent destruction of our planet but can't seem to define when or how that will happen should not use the law to force me to pay taxes to accords, treaties, and agreements which accomplish little more than to put money in the hands of government and its bureaucrats. Planned Parenthood should not be able to use my tax dollars to engage in an activity that I and many others have defined as murder. No matter the amount of shouting down, the morally conservative slice of this country will never see it as anything else. This is an excellent example of government picking winners, and getting more of something once they subsidize it. Planned Parenthood should be able to have a voice and try to convince me that it's not murder, but they shouldn't be able to use government money to subsidize this activity which will always be controversial and hotly debated. Same goes for crisis pregnancy centers. They should use the means that they have at their disposal to try and convince mothers to not abort their babies, but not use the government to further their agenda in this hotly debated and highly controversial subject. I take strong stances, but I see both sides of the argument.

Let's talk about voting rights now. It's a common practice nowadays for reporters to approach people on the street and ask them basic questions about

American government, and to juxtapose their lack of an answer with their ability to answer pop culture questions. My life is not impacted when an imbecile can name all of the Kardashian sisters but not the three branches of government. My life is impacted (albeit not as drastically as some would make it out to be) when that person helps to vote a bad person into office. Just like the removing of voting rights for welfare recipients, I think the voting public should be expected to answer/explain the fundamental tenets of our government, its branches and their responsibilities, and how voting in one person over the other would impact legislation on any issue. Point is, registering to vote could become a more involved process where someone would have more to do than simply entering their name and address on a form. This would remove the ability of someone to vote against Trump just because a celebrity they love shouted "Fornicate Trump!" on the television. Lest thou think I'm only looking to remove liberals, progressives, and democrats from the equation, look at the fact that folks of those ilk are more likely to dominate schools and college campuses, where you're supposed to learn that the three branches of government are in fact, not the olive, the Snooky, and the Santa Maria.

It's also no secret that government officials follow money. Campaign funding and political contributions should just simply stop. I've stated above that anyone running for an office with even a minor modicum of power should not be recompensed for their service with money. On top of making important decisions that affect the lives of others, the power attached to such an office, they already have enough perks.

The government could encourage those who are entering elected offices to form business partnerships and investments which will provide salary for their term of office. Taxpayer revenue could pick up the slack for reasonable lodging, transportation, leisure, and food, with the proviso that the people you represent would decide what's "reasonable" and if they say you need to sell your mansion, forego that expensive trip to the Bahamas, and do without caviar and champagne on your birthday, so be it. You're a public servant. Now serve. The information age has shown us just how fast we can communicate. I'd see no problem in a congressman asking his constituency in the morning of a slow work day if he is allowed to take his family to an exclusive and luxurious restaurant that night, providing reasons why it can be afforded on the taxpayer's dime and showing that a reasonable period of time has elapsed since their last extravagant outing. We are their bosses, after all. Any highly skilled, low skilled, salary, or hourly government worker should retain their wage. Any government official who has the legislative, judicial, or executive power to influence and order the lives of others can serve the public without wage. This would increase the spirit of altruism and not self-serving...um...ness in our elected politicians.

When it comes to saving our country money and getting out of debt, abolishment of politician wages will be more than just a drop in the bucket.

They should also not be allowed to accept contributions. There are so many laws, so much debate, so many scandals, so many people in prison, and so much controversy over contributions that it all just needs to be stopped. A predetermined amount of money (yes, taxpayer money) should be set aside for each qualified candidate in a race. The bigger the race, the bigger the stakes, the bigger the amount. They should be told to spend it wisely, and then be allowed to disseminate it as they see fit, providing proof of spending it within the rules once the race is over. There are so many private citizens engaging in campaigns completely independent of the candidates as it is, there will be no shortage of outside help. Their money just shouldn't be put in the hands of candidates. Shenanigans too often ensue once that happens. Contributions are like a wonderful toy that one kid uses the way it was meant to be while a couple brats use it to beat the responsible kid over the head. So it just should be abandoned until humans are no longer corrupt (not bloody likely, I know). Once campaign contributions no longer are a tax write off and taxpayer money is what candidates are held accountable for using responsibly, the general populace won't have a problem with the abolishment of this system.

While elected officials are elected to represent the people in their voting areas, they do also have to follow their conscience in voting. This often leads to them voting differently than what the majority of their constituency believes. And that's perfectly fine, so long as a principled stand on clearly defined morals is followed. Disagree or not, I respect courage of convictions. Were we to abolish the two parties, this practice will actually become less controversial. Too often people are expected to vote the party line so as to maintain power or push through legislation. This mentality weakens the idea of voting with your convictions. As I stated above, instantaneous access to information allows the informed voter to vote with candidates they can truly support without having to tolerate the nonsense that comes with party distinctions. Along with that instantaneous access could come unofficial polling of a person's constituency through electronic means. Mass email campaigns and websites like Survey Monkey were set up to streamline the old school practice of phone calls, which often inconvenience and take up people's time at the wrong time of the day. Now, a duly elected official can cast a poll on Twitter and within hours see how a good number of people they represent feel on an issue. So they can go to tools like this for positive information and data gathering, instead of using it solely for throwing hypercritical barbs at their opponents. When an official goes against their electorate in a voting or legislation measure, they can also use digital tools to justify their choices. It'd be a modern version of the fireside chat (the removal of this from standard practice

I count as a great loss), and a check to their power is possibly being removed from office when they are up for reelection if they go against the electorate too often for what are perceived as weak reasons.

Increase a measured amount of transparency in government programs. I don't subscribe to the Julian Assange anarchical mode of transparency. Government should keep some secrets to keep us safe. But government agencies, programs, and departments should have total and utter financial transparency. Were I president, I'd make every government agency justify themselves and their continued existence based on the tangible need they fill and the measurable benefits they provide. The Federalists believed in a strong government, not a big one. The difference being that a strong government makes sound and moral decisions for the greater good. A big government continually invades areas of people's lives and continues to grow even if the need, real or perceived, is fulfilled or taken away. Hard conversations need to be had with a lot of agencies and whether or not they are still needed. If they are continued, they should have full and total transparency in reporting how they are using taxpayer money. Many school districts do this in good faith to show they haven't violated the public trust, or when they have been forced to by oversight when it has become apparent they are reckless, irresponsible, or corrupt in their spending of taxpayer dollars. I'd have no problem if websites were set up to show the budget, expenses, and spending of every government agency.

Accountants and interested parties in other agencies and across this land could not only find and report discrepancies and recklessness but provide solutions to how they can better manage money that was not earned, but rather coerced from the people. The more checks on power there are the less likely it is for that power to be abused, and money wasted or spirited away to serve a wicked person's ends.

Guns

YEAH, I'M NOT even going to touch this one...yet. That makes the title of my book a lie. I'm a shyster. A crook. A flim-flam man. If you're angered by that, feel free to return the signed copy I handed to you, as I'm sure these are the only copies in circulation at this point.

Ok let me give at least one area of this multifaceted debate a go. Mass shooters love gun-free zones more than Hitchcock loved platinum blondes, more than Trump loves rhetorical Twitter diarrhea, more than Californians love hearing their roads and highways name-dropped in songs and movies, more than Troy Aikman and Joe Buck love Aaron Rodgers' improvisation skills, more than the French love inscrutable film endings, more than the author of this book loves irritating and distracting asides. Among gun-free zones shooters love are schools. Mind you, this idea isn't even original with me. It just makes too much sense for it ever to be implemented in these illogical times. I don't think it's too cheesily poetic to say that children are our greatest natural resource, as they are the ones that will be filling jobs, working careers, and leading the country when we are all so old as to be dependent on prune juice to keep regular. Along with the military reduction I suggest elsewhere, there are a lot of active duty members and former military who struggle to stay employed who would love to be employed to protect our children. I'd say along with locks, alarms, drills, and similar safety measures, a couple of riflemen with necks as thick as their heads stationed outside each point of egress for the school day would be an effective deterrent from anymore school shootings occurring. We've got a lot of schools, but also a lot of soldiers in this country willing to serve and protect. We use them to protect politicians, our money, places containing hazardous materials, top secret facilities, airports, train stations, those free-loaning aliens living rent-free at Area 57, and other crowded areas. Why not schools? Goodness sakes, schools employ unarmed security guards. Soldiers and policemen patrolling the outside and inside of school campuses could pull double duty as security guards. If I ever run for president I hope the preceding sentence, in effect suggesting we put some people out of work, doesn't get me in trouble with the influential security guard PAC. They have a lot of clout. But I digress.

Vigilance is the price of safety and freedom. Since we are living in difficult times and the generally agreed upon value of human life is rapidly declining (people who believe AND ACT like everyone else is made in the image of God have been actively fighting against this decline for ages) and it's indescribably stupid to try and *educate* mental health problems away; education only being a remedy for indigence, not immorality, and even um...biggerly stupidness...to assume we can stop and fix all cases of errant mental health in time, I guess we have to go the populist route and do what works, not what is pretty. Maybe in time we'll figure out that this isn't just a mental health problem, and we might admit as a people that we are sinful on top of being sick. But I dream.

Oh, and one more thing while we are firmly perched on hobby horses. Liberals are fond of pointing out that mass shooters are mostly white. Fair point. In response, conservatives are fond of pointing out that urban murderers are mostly non-white. Also a fair point. However, maybe the finger pointing is not doing anything but feeding racism, prejudice, division, resentment, and bitterness among a people that are all part of one nationality and should be working together to fix problems. But I pontificate.

Business

OUR GOVERNMENT HAS a lot of work to do. That's why that part of this annoyingly wordy book is long and detailed. Business has some change to do also. As I've stated before, I see both sides of an argument, and often fall in the middle, either ideologically or in the nature of the solution. Those who chronically argue without offering solutions just want to hear themselves speak.

Tucker Carlson, if nothing else, is fantastically entertaining for someone who aspires to live life through their intellect and not their emotions. He gathers folks from the lunatic fringe of progressivism and uses the Socratic method to get them to embarrass themselves. I believe this sets him above some of the other Fox News guys, because they argue and criticize. Carlson is more dignified, and uses questions to trap his guests. Neil Cavuto is even better at calmly trapping a person in their own arguments. Carlson sometimes tends to laugh and deride his guests. Cavuto doesn't typically do this, thereby preserving their dignity. Even though Carlson got his start on a crossfire show, their shows hearken back to the civilized debate that existed before the crossfire format shows that became so popular in the late nineties and 2000's.

They've both had young people (often in line with Bernie Sanders' philosophies of government) come on and argue for free college tuition, higher minimum wage, and destruction of rape culture on college campuses. I've got a solution to all three of these problems; one that can satisfy both sides.

I'm with Bernie Sanders. There I said it. Well, let me back up a bit. I'm with Bernie Sanders as pertains the one issue of student loan debt. There I said it in more specific terms. Heads exploded yet, conservatives? I am feeling a small portion of the Bern. Maybe just enough to singe my eyebrows. I *do* want to cancel all student loan debt. Not because this is the right thing to do, certainly not. I am still struggling with whether or not it's the right thing to do. I want to do it because it'll correct the unacceptable and unsustainable status quos of this system.

I, like millions of others, was tricked as a young adult into saddling my future, more tired, rapidly aging, and increasingly lonely self into a large amount of student loan debt. I also don't think government should take on student loan debt. That would entail a massive tax increase. I think they should just cancel it. Yes, this will show all these poor graduates that their actions don't always have consequences, but it will also wildly improve their credit scores, so you take the good with the bad. This will also entail government overstepping their authority by a million-cagillion-plus-infinity-plus-one country miles. It's why as a conservative I'm so conflicted about it. But I'm rationalizing it by the fact that schools are engaging in deceptive practices in tricking students to take the loans, demanding they take multiple years of expensive classes they don't need for their future career (classes which are often quite awesome but should be reserved for those who can afford them) and leaning on the government to keep them afloat in the short term until the student is able to start paying them back. It's the biggest and most elaborate scam ever perpetrated on a totally willing mark. The world's best hucksters running long cons could take notes. A massive government cancellation will result in some colleges shutting down, and the ones that survive this purge will understand that from here on out, they will need to make their profits in more honest and transparent ways, while also coming to terms with the fact that they will simply make less profit for the foreseeable future. If some PHD's get downsized in the process and some residence halls are boarded due to smaller student bodies, so be it. The lesson will be duly, albeit harshly learned.

It's a travesty of travesties that we will trick an 18-year old trying to live better and more comfortably than the conditions they grew up in into accepting tens (sometimes hundreds) of thousands of student loans against the abstract commodity of knowledge, instead of a few thousand dollars to start up or invest in small businesses, which typically have physical commodities that can be reclaimed if the investee defaults. The overhauling of minimum wage and traditional business practices I propose below will also help us fix this problem.

Free college tuition doesn't really work. Government already pays for free public primary and secondary education. There's a group of people who are able to recognize how poorly that is turning out. I call them the "Eyes and Ears Open and Functioning Properly Crowd". You may have heard of them. Post-secondary educational debt is at an all-time high with no reduction in sight. It's another reason why progressives say that the system is rigged. Government and loan agencies basically can trap you for life (or at least a large chunk of it) through subsidized and unsubsidized student loans. Someone has to pay for education, and I don't think the government is that someone. Rich, private individuals can't entirely pay for it, as redistributing their wealth will make it run out at some point, along with their inclination to earn it. I think this is where business can solve this problem.

The military and General Motors models can be altered slightly and applied here. General Motors says that if you give them 30 years of faithful service, they will pay you a collectively bargained pension and health benefits until you die. This used to allow someone the chance to step into the shop at age 18, forego college, and potentially retire comfortably at age 48. This model has been altered by changes to the industry, concessions made by the UAW in 2007, and a diminished U.S. workforce, but is still in place to some degree. The military says that if you give them 4 years of faithful service, they will give you $40,000+ in school tuition. If you give them 20 years of faithful service, they will give you an attractive pension and health benefits until you die. Like Thomas Paine said, honest men engaging in trade do more for this world than all the crowned ruffians that ever lived. Let's apply this model to business. Here's my plan:

Stop criticizing big corporations and start utilizing their resources. Social justice warriors love to bemoan the humongous conglomerates that dominate the business world, and the plight of the ma and pa operations that are dying off. These corporations hold tremendous financial power and political clout. One reason small operations are dying off is that we have so many laws that govern business. Only corporations can afford to pay exorbitant licensing fees, retain lawyers, and have research teams keep them on top of current laws. Ma and Pa have drastically fewer assets and you can't monetize pluck and gumption. A semi-conspiracy theorist might conclude based on lobbying and other factors that corporations try to keep laws stringent, insurance legislation intact, and minimum wages high because these things make running a small business not worth it for many. But that's just me using the logic I should have learned in school were Logic not forlornly staring in through the classroom windows at a party they were originally invited to but embarrassingly bounced. I've already addressed lobbying (it should be outlawed) and insurance (it should be drastically changed to allow the little guy to get ahead), and now, the minimum wage.

Zero out the minimum wage. Oh yes, I went there. Put your torches and pitchforks away. You'll see why eventually. The minimum wage is a hotly debated item. When people who work low-skilled jobs get their demand for higher wage, they get criticized by conservatives, fired by their bosses, or replaced by machines. While I am compassionate to those who suffer due to low wages, I tend to lean toward the Republican side of this argument.

This is because I've worked minimum wage jobs before I was acquired skills through experience and college. I've worked two minimum wage jobs at once. I've worked higher than minimum wage jobs since I graduated college. I've made more than minimum wage running my own business. I've lost money on jobs running my own business. I've also worked a minimum wage job in order to make extra cash while working my higher-than-minimum job. I've been in all sorts of situations. This I do know. If you want to make livable wage, you need to increase your output.

It seems harsh, but I've been perfectly happy working two jobs that expected something at least in the neighborhood of an eight-hour work day. I have been happy because I know I'm providing for those I love, and I know that if I save my money I can change my situation in the future. This is something the folks clamoring for a $15 minimum don't seem to understand. There are twenty-four hours in the day. We Americans, due to our comfort and luxury, tend to break the day into three eight-hour chunks; work, leisure/personal, and sleep. Problem is this doesn't gel with what humans had to do for thousands of years before the industrial age introduced us to said comfort and luxury. Sunup to sundown was the norm in agricultural times, when the work day was dictated by the job needing done, not the mutually agreed upon bare minimum.

Just because we are used to a different norm doesn't mean we are entitled to it. I tell my kids, my students, my peers, anyone who will listen to me; The world doesn't owe you anything. Once you start down the path of entitlement, there is no end to what you think you and your existence are to have bestowed by the effort of others. President Lincoln's second inaugural address, enshrined in the wall of his memorial, has something to say about men who would make their bread off the backs of others. I know through my experience there's almost no problem that can't be solved by a little (or a lot) of work.

So that's one reason I don't advocate for

government increasing the minimum wage. Those who wish to get ahead can just choose to work harder and work more. Low skilled, low wage jobs, in a perfect world, would be entirely populated by teenagers, college kids, skilled workers looking for extra cash, and bored retirees looking for something to do beyond arguing with their wives and feeding the ducks. Maybe even a small contingent of unskilled adults who are okay with flatlining at a certain life station. Problem is what we have now is twenty-somethings, thirty-somethings, and forty-somethings who have decided to treat a job like a career but then turn around and get mad when their wage doesn't support increasing costs of living, often extravagant and luxurious at that. Ever seen an obese person with a smartphone argue they aren't making a livable wage? Their physical state and that computer in their pocket have curb-stomped their own argument. They aren't okay with flatlining at a certain life station but are okay without increasing their output. They don't know or don't acknowledge that an engine can't pick up speed without higher RPM's.

Another reason is that rising wage does affect the price of things. Whether or not the increases in minimum wage over the years has stayed steady with the rising prices of consumer goods and services, one cannot deny that the price of things has risen steadily since the advent and increase of minimum wage. This is not the best reason, but it is a reason.

Another reason is that I think we could enter an employee market, much like we had back in the heyday of the car industry. Think about it. Companies who lower their wage to charity work won't ever have anyone work for them. Companies who raise their wages and benefits will always have workers ready to work for them. It's why GM has had to perform lotteries for employment for many years. They simply had so many applicants they weeded many of them out with an unbiased system. The <u>unskilled</u> worker who works for McDonald's will more than double their wage and benefits doing <u>unskilled</u> work for GM. Yes, they collectively bargained this with their union, but the market value of the car industry demanded increases anyway, once the wickedness of management was addressed with the labor strikes. Point is, companies should be competing for workers, instead of workers competing for work. And when a worker finds another, better job due to their experience and skills, said companies should be happy for them. We live in an age when the bad actions of a person or company can be disseminated to the world with the click of a button. Any company who mistreats or lowers wages unfairly will not be around very long without changing.

Get government involved to a certain extent. Here's where the aforementioned resources of corporations could be put to good use. Using the model of the military, we could zero out the minimum wage, corporations could start employing young people in their teenage years when they don't have to pay for their room and board, and the hours they devote to the company could be banked towards time spent in college, trade school, apprenticeships, or small business investments/startups/latch-ons. They could do this for a mutually-agreed upon amount of time (high school kids working evenings, weekends, and summers), then get their reward at the end of their tenure, just like the military. Once they finish their commitment, the money they've banked could be put towards the expense of learning the skills necessary for a career with the aforementioned college, trade schools, apprenticeships, or small business investments. The subsequent positions they get in said careers will pay for the time when they are young adults who want to move into their own places, drive their own cars, and pay their own bills. If a young person decides to forego college/trade school/apprenticeship, the company could give them a cash payout, or (better yet) help get them set up in a small business. I cut lawns and trees for a living. You can make excellent money doing this and you don't need a college degree. The trades pay better than many college degree jobs. You don't need to spend four years learning to be a carpenter. Any money banked but not spent can be used to help the young person get set up in their trade, buy a car, rent an apartment, purchase food, pay bills, get caught up in an expensive drug habit, etc.

One necessary offshoot of this revolutionary form of business is that the age of legal adulthood will probably have to be changed. Right now, I have a nineteen-year-old in college. So long as she stays in college, I can claim her as a dependent until the age of twenty-three. However, I can no longer take advantage of the child tax credit which has paid off so many of my bills over the years. As kids go at their own pace (according to my paradigm of education below) to enter the workforce, parents may have to take an extended tax allowance and child tax credit for supporting them. This might even be a non-issue for the most brilliant kids who finish high school at such an early age (according to my paradigm for education below) that they enter the workforce, and all of their future educational accounts are settled by age eighteen. I say we change the age of legal adulthood (and legal voting age also) to compensate for more kids living at home into young adulthood while banking commercial money for their professional futures.

Actually, we could make the legal voting age different for everyone. Those who have finished the prerequisite steps for reaching and maintaining the responsibilities necessary for adulthood should be rewarded with an early voting age. Something like a year of independent living, budgeting, and responsible legal choices is a start. Those who are a little bit behind should have their voting rights withheld until they can attain a comparable level of personal and professional maturity. The cookie-cutter approach of eighteen doesn't at all account for the individual differences which render such an approach laughable, nor does it compensate for statistical differences, which overwhelmingly show that we men don't really enter adult maturity until a couple years after our female counterparts. A personal voting age based on choices in the teenage years can be an encouragement for we males to step up and mature in the corporate sense. More importantly, it can be used as an incentive for the brightest and most brilliant among us to stay the course and be ahead of the curve, while being a promise withheld for a measure of time for those who struggle on the path to maturity.

A personalized voting age might actually result in the young people who struggle in the core academics in school achieving a lower statistical voting age than their university-bound counterparts. Think about it. Under my educational plan, which you haven't read yet, but will, unless you get sick of corny interruptions and unnecessary rabbit trails, these folks would be entering the trades and acquiring lucrative careers while the teachers' pets are still at university living off scholarships, mommy and daddy's dime, and money banked with jobs they worked leading up to the transition to college. Worth respect, but not what you'd exactly call independent living. Their reward is farther down the road than those who chose a less-specialized career. And since those who work with their hands tend to vote more conservatively than their liberal university counterparts, this will be one more step in my evil plan to subjugate this entire land under crushing Republican control (insert evil laugh and evil fart).

As a young person banks time for their respective company, they should be able to withdraw at reasonable intervals for movies, dates, walking around money, small vacations, getting caught up in an expensive drug habit, and the sort, with the understanding that they will have to make that time up at a later time. This will introduce them to a concept similar to credit cards. It also will show them the idea that almost every action in life is an investment for the future, or a withdrawal for the present. It's those people who always withdraw for the present who end up on the losing end of life. It's part of why I don't subscribe to the "live in the moment" philosophy. I'm playing the long game.

What's more, young people should be able to work for multiple companies during this banking time. Think about it. If you, as a fifteen-year-old entered an Old Navy store and were told that for the next four years, you'd be folding shirts that customers will continually pull out of place but not put back, you might want to shoot somebody and then shoot the gun that you used with another gun. If you, as a teenager are told that you'd spend six weeks doing that, then go work in a manufacturing plant with robots and machinery for another six weeks, then flip burgers for six weeks, then work on cars for six weeks, then answer phones for six weeks, then shelve library books for six weeks, then hang drywall for six weeks, then drive tractors and bale hay for six weeks, then usher theater patrons to their seats for six weeks, then and then and then (you get the point) you'd inspire all but those who are in severe need of unchanging routine, who should have the option of staying in a workplace they like. This worker exchange idea will not only allow kids to come to peace with working some jobs that are monotonous and repetitive with less-than-perfect supervisors, but it'll also give them experience in fields they may not choose as a career, but possibly a hobby. It'll also save them money in the future when they don't have to pay a guy to do something they already know how to do. See the episode of *The Simpsons* where Homer saves for an expensive kitchen makeover but feels emasculated by another man coming into his house and doing the work for him. In addition, they might get exposed to something they terribly enjoy, and end up changing the entire direction of their life before they've ever incurred a penny's worth of college debt. You're welcome, future kids. It was my idea first.

What's even more, we'd end the employer's market we've dis-enjoyed for quite some time now. Companies would be competing for the best workers, so their added perks (ex. meals, actual wage on top of banked money for the future, transportation to work, room and board allowances, facilitating your getting caught up in an expensive drug habit, etc.) would be a way to ensure they are getting the best workers (or hold lotteries if the overall quality of available workers rises beyond easily discernible discretion), while still ensuring those who are behind in terms of maturity and industriousness will still be able to work for the companies that have fewer resources to offer perks. One unfortunate offshoot of the need for equal opportunity is that many have (in a socialist mindset) perverted that idea to mean that outcome must needs also be equal. Outcome will never be equal, as humans are never equal in all ways and means. Were we to redistribute the wealth of all the rich, as the poorly veiled rhetoric shows that many American socialists clearly want, five years' time would show tremendous inequalities of wealth again. People make different choices, desire different levels of extravagance and luxury, have different connections, have different skills, are caught up in less expensive drug habits, and dare I say it, different levels of marketable intelligence and skills. So either regular and routine redistributions would be necessary to stay in line with the propositions of Socialism, or we just don't do that in the first place. I vote for the latter. All in agreement say "Aye". The moneyless world of *Star Trek* can't even be used as an example, as some people in that world are lofty and laudable starship captains, and some are redshirted ensigns whose job it is to absorb some of these pesky phaser blasts being thrown around at an alarming rate. Socialists who want the former, continue reading this book quietly without an angry external emotional display, if you're even capable of such a thing. The ayes have it.

People over thirty love to bemoan the general faults of this generation. Too much time on social media, not enough interpersonal skills, entitled, lazy, lower reading skills, expensive drug habits, blah blah blah. I tend to shy away from this because every generation has done this. Every generation looks at the up and coming kids and pontificates about things not being so "in my day". When my father was twelve years old, he was able to fix broken systems on a car, and even helped his dad pull out an engine and install a new one on the family truck. When I was twelve years old, I could beat Super Mario Brothers 3. So, yeah. Every generation has something to look down on the next one for, and our collective generational skills are declining. I could look down on kids today for using their phones too much, but I know that I do the same thing, just not to the same degree. Plus, I know that sin has always been around, and no generation was perfect or completely all good. My worker exchange idea and my ideas in a later chapter for education should result in the most highly skilled generations of kids entering adulthood until America ends. Point is, companies can network together and make the unskilled labor we all must face as youngsters more appealing through worker exchange programs.

As long as everyone keeps up their end of the bargain, we'll see a remarkable change in business and culture. Small and large companies alike could contribute by listing their jobs as "career", "stepping-stone", and "unskilled". For anyone they employ in the third category, they could be part of the worker exchange program along with doing their small part of paying for college for low-skilled workers. There could also be a governing body that oversees "stepping-stone" job listings to make sure that these are jobs that can and might lead to lucrative careers. This will make sure companies aren't able to sneak "unskilled" jobs into this category. There could be checks and balances in a system like this. Workers who are terminated from a job should be able to transfer their time banked, as a few moments of being a bad employee shouldn't outweigh days, weeks, and months being a good one. In addition, workers should have options for reporting on the environment, treatment, perks, and benefits of working for a specific company. This will raise accountability for them in return. In business terms, all the things I've described are win-win. Yes, there will be hiccups, necessary tweaks, growing pains, corruption, fraud, expensive drug habits, and such because you can't stop humans from being evil. What you can do is encourage them to be better. Money is a fantastic way to do that. Future money is a fantastic way to make sure we behave for the present. I get paid every Friday at my current job. I'm counting on my employer to pay me for time banked the week before. That keeps me from running around giving noogies and wet willies to my coworkers who are so very much asking for it when they get on my nerves. Money years down the road will serve as an enticement to good choices, eliminate the need to go into debt, and work wonders in our culture. We need to change the current system so as to encourage everyone involved to make everyone else involved as much money as possible so everyone involved can have a better life and enjoy more expensive drug habits.

So let's recap. This solves the minimum wage debate. This solves the college tuition and student loan debt debate (once this generation's debt is either paid or forgiven). The rape and debauchery culture (which stem from too much time on the hands of kids who are living on someone else's dime) on college campuses can be fought by accountability measures like "hey kid, take twenty-two credits instead of twelve in order to get your tuition money dispersed" (idle hands being the devil's plaything). This solves the declining generational skill debate. What will old-timers and grey heads complain about now? I'm sure they'll find something. This solves the corporate conglomeration versus ma and pop debate. This solves the employer's market debate. This solves the problem of kids who don't want to do college but still want to make good money debate (Mike Rowe et. al, you're welcome). This solves the problem of kids getting into jobs but not doing their best because they have no incentive to do their best. This will (not immediately, but eventually) solve the problem of the millions of 20-40 year olds who treat low-skilled jobs as careers. This doesn't solve the debate of is-Lebron-or-is-Jordan-the-G.O.A.T., but I don't know that we'll ever solve that one.

Education

IT'S BROKEN. WE all know that but can't agree how to fix it. In the process, we lose sight of whom we should be holding responsible to fix it. Government, teachers, superintendents, districts, and the workers of the industry shouldn't be the only ones tasked with fixing education. Families and students also should. When I have a menial task to accomplish at home, I can often delegate that task to my teenagers. This frees me up to finish something they can't do. For instance, I keep my personal question banks for my English classes on a website called Schoology. It's a fantastic resource, but putting the questions from the textbooks into question banks is a long and tedious process. So, I give my Teacher's Edition to my eldest son and daughter, instruct them on how to phrase each question for each activity, and let them go on their merry way. They don't like it, but they don't have to. They know that a family with one parent can accomplish more with division of labor, not this atrocious paradigm of a single parent who tries to be the cool parent and lets their kids run the house. They respect, honor, and obey their father, so they do the task. That means I have the time to hook up my trailer, drive to a customer's house, and use my riding mower to cut their lawn. These are tasks they can't do. Division of labor is a beautiful thing. This idea should be applied to education. Schools don't produce strong or weak students. Families do. So families should be responsible for fixing schools. Teachers, administrators, and politicians will also have their part to play. Here's how.

Cut out all summer school and credit recovery programs. These are a joke. Government is the only consumer who pays for a service provider (in this case a student) to fail for nine months, and then pays for that person to spend five weeks in a summer school program, possibly fail again, and then pays for that person to sit in front of a computer for a prerequisite number of hours "recovering" their credits. If you, as a McHungry consumer, drove your McVehicle to the drive-through at McDonalds and ordered McNuggets and they gave you a McBurger instead, you McWouldn't McPay a McSecond McTime for McThem to McGget your McFirst McOrder McRight. I'll stop now. When they mess your order up a second time, you wouldn't throw your hands up in the air and say "Well, let me pay a third time." That's foolishness. Government does this though. They pay for a kid to goof off (thereby stressing teachers out and bogging down the system), pay for them to take summer school, and then pay for the kid to recover in an even easier way. Ladies and gentlemen, what logical sense does it make for us to make things incrementally easier on a fool? Shouldn't that fool at some point feel the sting of their atrocious choices? Isn't life going to teach that fool something much harsher if we don't put our foot down, violently yank the hemi-powered engine out of the War Rig, and thunder at them "RICTUS!!!"...I mean..."ENOUGH!"? On my love of soft-and-somewhat-runny French Toast, I wish the logical human being wasn't an endangered species.

The solution is simple. At some point, a child who will not get with the program should be fiscally responsible (re: their parents should be fiscally responsible) for their continued education. If they can't pay, then homeschool or working for the school (if we are talking about a teenager) is an option. Seriously, I think that if students act a metaphorical mess at school, they can clean up a literal mess. If their parents have a problem with it, they can take their wild child somewhere else. But many parents who want their child to straighten up will be perfectly fine with them pulling duty as a janitor. I know I would were my student a knucklehead. This would get the problem child away from the classroom he/she so desperately desires to disrupt, teach them how to do hard and unenjoyable work, and encourage them to straighten up and fly right. Point is, school is not here to coddle a young person's feelings and preserve their sense of self-esteem whenever they make horrific choices. In fact, the earlier a school (maybe even the parent) gives consequences for said choices, the earlier the child will learn to enter civilization and act appropriately. This will clean up much of the problem of young adults (mostly men) entering adulthood with no marketable skills and resorting to crime to make money.

In addition, it will clean up much of the bullying and harassment that is so insidiously tolerated in schools in the name of "second chances" and keeping numbers up so as to maintain funding. Much of this behavior comes from academically unsound students who are bored or in over their heads in the classroom. Nature abhorring a vacuum, as it is wont to do, very rarely means they fill their time with constructive behavior. Bullies don't understand or respond to appeals to their better nature. They have no better nature. That's what makes them a bully. The power they feel while bullying is intoxicating, and we all know children don't know how to control baser experiences like intoxication. Bullies only understand force equal to or greater than the force they are applying. Steeper consequences will compel students who can be reasoned with to stop or never engage in it in the first place, along with removing more quickly— funding be damned—those who do engage in it from the school environment. Title IX was put in place particularly to protect young girls in school from discrimination and intimidating practices. We can't fully eliminate human evil with education or legislation. We can only restrain it with best practices and consequences. This is particularly true when it comes to gender differences. Young women need protection from aggressive, evil young men, and they are not getting it in the way things are currently going. The standard progressive answer is to say "just teach young men to respect women," as if it's that easy. A school has very little to do with the formation of appropriate behavior in the moral sense for a child. They, especially since religious thought is restrained in schools, typically have to do with the formation of appropriate behavior in the practical sense; that is, how to maintain one's good standing in the public forum. But this practical education doesn't engage the heart in a profound meditation on the good. Educating moral behavior is the family's job. Even when families fail, schools (as all evidence clearly points out) are ill-equipped to mold and release upon the world the morally upright adult.

"Free public education is a right" you say? "Students and parents shouldn't have to pay" you say? Okay. Maybe that part of our government needs to be changed. The part about something that many students refuse to take advantage of being an entitlement. Free education is the privilege of those who take advantage of the right. For others, it's just seven hours of babysitting. Seriously, have you looked at reading curriculum from colonial times, when free public education wasn't a right? It's on a higher level. When parents made a conscious choice to have lettered children, those children went to school with at least some built in respect, if not an altogether higher value of education, the education was better, and the expectations were higher. Joe Clark, the venerated principal played by Morgan Freeman in *Lean on Me*, would say that it's not the school's job to rescue those who don't care. It's the family's. If the schools stopped taking on this Sisyphean task, the families (of all shapes and sizes) would be forced to step up and do their jobs. There needs to be a shift in philosophy about why a school actually is here.

Schools have got to get it in their head that, despite being a parent-in-place for a set amount of time, they are not a substitute parent. They are professionals running a place of professional business, providing a free but valuable service. This place is teaching a young person to dress up their behavior, communication, and interaction in order to survive in a world that places high demands on professionalism. Schools who make their kids feel "at home" are doing them a disservice. I ask students how they would feel if I came into their bedroom, kicked up my feet on their desk, ate a 3 Musketeers, stuffed the wrapper into a crevice despite easy access to a garbage can, chewed gum, stuck it to the bottom of their dining room table, and then caught an attitude when they took issue with all this. I tell them my classroom is not their home and they'd better act accordingly. This denotes a deep philosophical change that is the fault of parents and educators. For years, parents have allowed schools to act like fill-in parents, and schools have taken that opportunity to try and become too much to students. It becomes a vicious, self-feeding cycle that has resulted in a situation where it's nigh unto impossible to teach some students at all.

The other philosophical change schools need to embrace is the idea that they don't need to "keep numbers up." The advent of the charter school has made public schools compete for bodies. Homeschool and private schools weren't really taking away that much from public schools, as the parents of these students paid their taxes anyway. But charter schools have started making public schools suffer because they take larger numbers of kids away. This resulted in a mad scramble for carbon units. Metaphorically imagine people with master's degrees acting like Hungry Hungry Hippos. There is little to no regard for the quality of students. This mad scramble still goes on, and in some schools, is the main priority. You'll hear superintendents say things like "maintain attendance", "get numbers up", "recruit scholars". These are all epithets for the real concept at work; get the money attached to that child, no matter the cost to teachers' peace of mind or the quality of education students are getting. I know this is going on because I worked in a charter school, and have worked in many public schools where these conversations take place also. Scrambling for money makes a district lose sight of the quality that is paramount to sending productive citizens into the world. With wholesale philosophical and pragmatic changes to the education system, the schools who scramble for bodies will soon be recognizable to the rational person and easily exposed as corrupt and possessing of screwy priorities.

One reason school leaders throw at teachers for doing their best to keep numbers up is so that they don't have to reduce staff. This is fallacious reasoning for two reasons. One is that we currently have a teacher shortage nationwide. Turns out, when you make people go tens of thousands of dollars into debt, micromanage them, don't trust them to do their job without said micromanagement, pay them pittance when put up against the good they do for society, refuse to give them raises without test score results in spite of their dedication and loyalty from year to year, heap all kinds of non-negotiables and mandates on them, force them to teach to standardized tests instead of real critical thinking and problem solving skills, force them to continue their education through unending professional development and continuing college courses, don't advocate for them when conflicts arise with parents, AND allow the dummies of the student body to stress them out without any recourse or consequences, teachers tend to get burnt out and quit. The teaching field is a leader in the realm of those who leave the profession within five years. By the sword of Damocles, how I yearn for Logic to drop a comeback album.

The second reason is that teachers are working professionals. That phrase can only be applied to humans. Throughout their history, humans have had an uncanny knack for adapting to difficult situations. When teachers are laid off due to necessary reductions in staff, they usually don't give up on life. They do what working professionals do and go find professional work somewhere else. I've said this until I'm blue in the face to my coworkers. If my employer severs their professional relationship with me, I am then free to pursue employment with another employer. "Keeping numbers up" in the name of retaining staff silently implies that educational excellence no longer matters, or at least is a lower priority, along with not giving teachers the credit to go and find work elsewhere. This is the other reason we have a teacher shortage. A job that pays the bills but which you hate ends up feeling like a prison. You can't search for another job while you're at work, but are often so stressed out when you get home (along with having stacks of papers to grade) that the laborious process of job searching at home becomes all the more difficult. So teachers don't find other teaching jobs, because they don't believe the grass is greener in schools who have the same jacked-up priorities, so they end up leaving the industry, often for much more money and less stress. In a situation like that, the difference you're making in young people's lives pales in comparison. You can't put a price tag on peace of mind. Rest in peace, logic. We never really knew thee.

Demolish all standardized testing. Hear that? It's the collective cheer of real teachers everywhere reading these words. Standardized testing is a huge industry. But it only exists to make money for the professional development hucksters, keep curriculum administrators who don't really care about true education excellence in work, and to allow government bureaucrats to justify their existence. Teachers despise standardized testing. It takes away valuable instructional time. One-hundred-eighty school days are not really that when you account for standardized testing. That's not even mentioning the preparation for it, which includes sneaking in questions that students will see on tests into normal lessons. It's also leaving out the days that students take practice tests, tutoring in preparation for it (which teachers are often press-ganged into doing), meetings held in preparation for it, and all the stress that they put on schools. Schools with high test scores get funding. Schools with low test scores get extra training for their teachers, threats of being shut down, and less funding, thereby making it harder for them to retain good teachers, thereby making it harder to teach student bodies with struggles, thereby catching them in a cycle of trouble.

And for what? Standardized testing success isn't

causally linked to professional success. What's the return on investment? Not much, I'm afraid, especially when you consider the effort the adult world puts into finding the best individuals to suit their respective needs. Think about it. When a kid gets a great score on the ACT and SAT, he or she is given offers to attend prestigious colleges. When a kid gets an average score on the tests, they are given offers to attend less prestigious but nonetheless respectable colleges. When a kid gets a below average score on the tests, they are directed to attend community college. But their test scores are only part of the criteria. Their overall GPA, high school attendance record, and lack of legal trouble are also determining factors. One could argue it's more important because what you do over four years of high school is more important than a few days of testing. And when this kid gets an invitation to apply, and accepted, are they just accepted? Sometimes, not always. Sometimes, they have to take college entrance exams.

But wait, isn't that what standardized testing is supposed to be, a measuring stick for how college-ready they are? So, why are we doubling up on the examinations? Might as well ask why clouds are white, why the sun sets in the west, and why Kim Kardashian is famous. Just because. Oh, and so the aforementioned government bureaucrats can hold a cushy and powerful government job instead of joining the real workforce. So let's recap. Schools, paid for by taxpayers, have to issue standardized tests, all of the effort and resources for which are paid for by taxpayers, so they can show state government officials whose time and efforts are paid for by taxpayers that they've been doing their jobs effectively. Meanwhile universities and colleges, of which even the ones who accept state funding also find private enterprise means to fund their efforts, turn around and put in similar testing efforts to make sure young people who apply are going to be an asset to their organization. Sounds like someone is wasting their time. I'll go with the organization that takes all, not some of its revenue from taxpayers. This is an easy fix. Abolish all standardized testing. Let teachers teach their curriculum, which is supposed to be reading, writing, analytical thinking, and critical problem-solving skills, not the right bubble to fill in on a test. Let the colleges absorb the work of finding good candidates...which they are already doing. I feel like I'm in a time-loop. Doctor Sam Beckett, save me!

Bring back the classical education. Since you left high school, have you ever of your own volition picked up and read *The Last of the Mohicans*? *The Scarlet Letter*? *Paradise Lost*? *Dante's Inferno*? *The Iliad* and *The Odyssey*? "The Devil and Tom Walker"? Shakespeare? A fourth grade English primer from the 1700's? Any number of instantly recognizable classics that have been turned into much easier to understand movies? What's common among these works? Fill in the blank with your answer (or just skip ahead to mine) _____. They are tough reads. Are they tough reads because they make no sense? Of course not. David Lynch can take a hike as far as I'm concerned. They are tough reads because the language skills on display are so high, and our collective language skills have devolved, and are continuing to do so. Don't believe me? Ladies and Gentlemen of the jury, I submit for your consideration: LOL, BTW, OMG, R U gonna go 2 the party?, and so on. Call it my bias as an English teacher, but we are rapidly becoming linguistic imbeciles. The classical education, and objective standards of what constitutes great writing need to be put back in their rightful place. We live in an age of self-esteem where objective standards of beauty and art are all but gone, and you can't tell someone who threw excrement against pictures of vaginas that what they do isn't art because they'll shout you down with screams of "FASCIST!" and "I'm a provocateur and you just don't get it!"

In the time of Washington Irving and Nathaniel Hawthorne, young people were translating Greek at age six. They were graduating with a school diploma at age twelve, and finishing college at age eighteen. Not all of them, but many. And you can't even explain that away with the difference in life expectancy between then and now. They had a tougher curriculum to deal with than we do now. We continually dumb things down to play to the lowest common denominator, instead of heeding the wise words of Edward

James Olmos from *Stand and Deliver*, when he says "Students will rise to the level of expectations, Senior Molina."

Students back in colonial days had to learn Greek, Latin, French, German, philosophy, ethics, comparative religion, and logic. Outside of electives and college courses, much of those have passed by the wayside. Without Greek and Latin, students don't learn the foundations for much of our language. Without German and French, students don't get exposed to the two languages of vastly different style that helped shape ours. Nor do they get a leg up on conversing with people who have immense economic power the world over. Without philosophy, ethics, and religion courses, they don't understand how others of beliefs different than those outside their homes define right and wrong. Without logic, they don't come to the understanding of why their actions have consequences. They just float around, making choices, (sometimes) serving the consequences, and making the same choices without ever developing their character. I think I've mentioned logic once or thrice in these extravagantly adorned pages (editor's note: Mr. Roberts, while being a valued client, did not forward to our firm the extra monies for our Extravagantly Adorned Package, so he and his readers can deal with simple black print on white pages).

That's not even mentioning the inexcusable fact that our high school students aren't graduating fluent in Spanish, the foreign language it makes the most sense for them to be learning to mastery. In addition, they aren't studying Asian languages, the practical application of which cannot be overstated, primarily Mandarin and Japanese due to their respective economic influence. Also, students don't learn to speak Hebrew or Arabic, thereby furthering the already widening gap between our culture and the cultures of Asia Minor. Picking up a Slavic language like, oh, I don't know, RUSSIAN might help them in the aforementioned realm of economics. There are a myriad of languages practiced in the African continent, in addition to variations on French and Arabic. Students should also be required to learn an African continental language as Africa emerges in the realm of global influence and we strive to be better about teaching African history in our mainstream curriculums. This is all impossible? We're going to overload kids' brains? Where will we find the teachers? It is possible. There are many people who learn upwards of thirty to forty languages in their lives; it all starts with the nouns and verbs and expands from there. And Rosetta Stone. I rest my case.

Yes, the world speaks English. Yes, English is the language of money, international airports, and political discourse. But it's the inconsiderate redneck who arrogantly states "everyone else can learn English because we are the most powerful...blah blah blah." I can't even finish that sentence, it infuriates me so.

That type of thought is boorish, brainless, classless, and borderline bullying. It also doesn't prepare our students to be global citizens. Yes, nationalism is on the rise and cultures differ and all that, but we need to teach young people how to think critically and solve problems, not just with people who look and sound like them. With American exceptionalism becoming a thing of the past and the world catching up to our economic power, students need all the help they can get. Not in terms of keeping America number one, but making them as individuals more rounded and ready to work together to benefit everyone.

Long story short, the classical education, with some tweaks to fit the times, should make a comeback. In the time of Hawthorne those who we remember now were exceptional. I will concede that point. But we now have free education for all. So, with only a few examples of psychopaths who won't get with the unwritten rules of civilization, all students should be exceptional. A few minutes' drive from my house on the west side of Flint is a children's museum called Flint Children's Museum. Simple enough, right? The name explains what it is. On the wall of that museum is a quote I'm very fond of. "Every child is a potential genius." I've repeated it many times to anyone who will listen to my theories of education. Quite simply, when we start young and give students no choice but to be a genius, then geniuses they will be. I'll get to forcing students to excel in a later section.

Stop making attendance compulsory There are a lot of kids who just won't join society and live within the social contract. Even more tragic, many of their parents not only don't force them to do so, they are the ones who taught them their inappropriate social skills. Many of these kids don't attend regularly, nor do their parents make them, until losing their welfare benefits or calls from Child Protective Services become an issue. Then they make their kids attend, sometimes the minimal amount of time. Because these children come to school so far behind the curve, bereft of appropriate social and focus skills, and only looking to have fun during their school day, they bog the system down. They spend their time in classrooms disrupting instruction, acting a mess during individual/group work time, and earn their way out of the classroom and into the principal's office more often than not. They often don't understand what they did wrong because our culture (including our schools) is constantly telling young people to "be yourself", "live your truth", or some such other foolish nonsense which doesn't account for the fact that when hundreds of civilized folk in one building don't like the self that you are being, it's not they who have the problem, it's you and the aforementioned self you are trying to be true to. Keep fighting the power, kid. See where it gets you.

These kids also commit the worst crime one can commit in school, barring physical violence or bullying. That is, detracting from the education from others.

They disrupt instructional and work time. Think about the time you saw this happen in a classroom. How many students told the kid to straighten up and took it upon themselves to correct them, and how many just sat there and watched it happen, allowing the teacher to do this? When instruction isn't happening, then the curriculum isn't moving forward. Make this happen enough times, and students learn less in the span of a year. Never did a young person say at the end of the year "Mr. Roberts, due to behavioral interruptions, school assemblies, snow days, standardized testing, and all the other foolish things schools do/allow to interrupt learning, we didn't get through the entire textbook, and I refuse to leave school until we do."

I say we stop making attendance compulsory. Leave welfare and CPS out of the equation. The government shouldn't give itself the power to take kids away from parents, unless criminal behavior or gross neglect come into the equation. Let the students who won't get with the program stay home. Eventually their parents will learn what a horrible mistake they've made in ruining their child and get that child on track, either with honey or vinegar, or a deftly nuanced combination of both. They can choose to homeschool their kid (nowadays parents don't even need to be that much of a teacher due to the multitudinous online programs available) or make sure they keep their nose clean when they do send them out into civilization. And this timeline of parents learning from their mistakes will be different for each family. Sometimes, it'll take less than a month of their child irritating the daylights out of them. Sometimes their little adult will have to enter adulthood and continue being a loser for it to happen. I've heard young men in my classroom say "I don't have to do my work. My ma said I can live with her as long as I choose." I believe them. There are moms who say this. Many are those who have had awful men come in and out of their lives so often that their son becomes a replacement because it's masculine love that can't leave. If they want to raise their children that way, let's as educators let them. The less that problem students are in the classroom, the better the classroom can move forward with those who have respect for authority, value learning, and want to excel in the professional world. This sounds heartless towards the problem children, but I've already addressed the philosophical shift that needs to happen in how schools view what they are and what they should be. In addition, life is full of second, third, fourth, fiftieth, and three-thousandth chances. Eventually, the majority of those kids will get with it.

There is the legal argument to consider here. Time and again, the courts have ruled that withholding a person's right to an education violates the fourteenth amendment protected right of life, liberty, and pursuit of happiness. Problem is that the "pursuit of happiness" clause has been extended to include pursuing an education so as to extend to personal comfort, luxury, possession, and leisure down the road. Here's the flaw in that thinking. Many students don't think about what's down the road. Many of them only think beyond the current moment, and they know they don't want to spend it conjugating verbs. By making attendance compulsory, we are actually taking away their pursuit of happiness. They are wildly unhappy in the formal school setting. Furthermore, taking away the compulsory factor isn't depriving them of their right. It's just giving them another option. Here is where the argument comes in "but government knows what is better for them". To that I would ask does government's foreknowledge supersede parental guidance and decision making? If a kid's parents don't care to send them to school consistently, and the kid is happier sitting at home losing round after round of *Fortnite*, I say let them. They will stop bogging down the system, and the parents will eventually learn what a horrible mistake they made, and force junior to get back on track, which is perfectly fine. Government can't force people to be intelligent and industrious. They can incentivize it but the decision has to be made in the heart first. The road to maturity is often bumpy, and arrival at the destination is different for everyone.

Now, short of condemning all knuckleheads for not falling in line, I will concede a certain contingent of the kids who just won't fall in line with education and its paradigms are actually not academically deficient. They are just uninterested in attaining a formal education.

Most kids who struggle in the core classrooms tend to struggle in life, but not all. I think our country and its businesses have to do some serious soul-searching regarding this. Forced attendance, forced adherence to school paradigms, and forced graduation from school to attain every adult job in this country just aren't necessary. I've interacted with many people in many walks of life who have shown proficiency in a myriad of skills that they didn't need to graduate high school in order to gain. Yes, brain surgeons and rocket scientists need formal education. But those are extremes in which only the most extraordinary intellects can actually achieve anyway. I didn't need school to teach me how to write this book. I just needed to read other, better by more competent writers. Whether or not formal education could have improved it is another matter, and one of little consequence because skill of language or lack thereof doesn't affect the lives of others. The guy who fixed my dryer last week didn't need deep understanding of the Bill of Rights and Federalist Papers to do so, just some mathematical and mechanical skills, all of which he picked up while apprenticing for eight months with an appliance repair professional. I'm an extrovert and I like to find out the life story of anyone who comes into my house, and I did, thereby keeping that guy from his next service call but engaging him in some delightful conversation. I could go on and on. There are some jobs which just don't need a high school diploma to perform at a high level. Government overreach has imposed a strangulating formula of forcing all kids to attend school, and that they all finish in order to move into the professional side of adulthood. Do away with it, says this humble writer, and you'll see people many teachers call "dummy" flourish and prosper.

To add to this point, compulsory attendance laws were argued for and put in place during the nineteenth century when the lack of child labor laws allowed for ten-year-olds to work sixty hours a week in dangerous textiles, mills, and manufacturing facilities for abysmal wages. Children who were younger than ten weren't even tracked statistically because it wasn't in the best interest of the employers to do so (and you think employers have too much power now?). Eventually the law caught up with the quickly evolving economy and shut down the abuses and injustices of the Industrial Revolution. Compulsory attendance once again became debated during the desegregation movement during the middle of the twentieth century as it was argued in segregated states that the state wouldn't have to be liable for the safety of black children who weren't forced to attend school. Desegregation and the Civil Rights bill fixed this perverse argument. These two arguments for compulsory attendance are outdated and their abuses taken away. Now, the argument for compulsory attendance is that a well-educated population is in the best interest of the nation. Opponents of it state that it rubs against the authority of a parent, who should be able to allow their child to be ignorant of academic matters.

These folks aren't making the best argument. I don't argue for abolishment of compulsory attendance so parents can be free to bestow the amazing gift of ignorance on their children. I argue for it so parents and children can choose the best path for their child. Many parents take their children out of public schools for homeschooling and private schools. Many parents who can't afford such options have no choice but to send their kid to public schools on at least a semi-regular basis. Many of these kids know their parents shall impose on them no conditions stricter than making sure they go enough to ensure the government doesn't bring down the hammer on their family. We are not doing these kids any favors by making them come to school and put on a show of learning. What we educators could be doing is allowing students such as these to enter the workforce under the condition that their path be one which leads to technical skills more marketable than minimum wage jobs. And that's not even to say we have to limit them to one, like the children I mention below who would start in ninth or tenth grade. If a child began at the age of ten learning a trade, they could have learned, apprenticed, and earned certification in two to four trades by the age of eighteen, allowing for on-schedule learning and faithful apprenticeship. The school could be responsible for him knowing the requisite reading, math, and science involved and the tradesmen working in conjunction (not employed by) the schools would be responsible for the rest, including the child's safety while under their care. I've no doubt incentives like funding, tax breaks, parental oversight and support, and waivers can be devised so tradesmen don't balk at the idea of having young ones in their places of work. Employers of the Industrial Revolution paid pittance to children because they knew they could get away with it. In a reversal of this abuse, the earlier a child is placed in a trade program, the *more* money they should be paid. They are, after all, leaving a comfortable school environment and most of the friends they've grown up with. This money can be saved in the worker program I discussed earlier in this book, and saved for business startups and the normal expenses young adulthood will expect of them.

Remember, revolutions begin with revolutionary ideas. Some radical ideas spring out of lunacy, but many are only seen as such in relation to established norms. If established norms aren't seeking and enacting the greatest benefit to the largest number of citizens, why keep them in place? Here's where I part ways with my conservative brethren. Conservatism is by nature resistant to change. While I admit I am conservative, that has more to do with my moral standards, which don't really change much once you've adopted a moral authority greater than yourself. Political conservatives must be willing to change once it's apparent governmental systems aren't producing the best potential results. In this case, they can be happy to change a failing system that is overseen and run by liberals anyway.

Track kids into careers early on so as to give them a taste while they still have time to change course. In fourth grade, much of the learning moves from conceptual to practical. Work becomes more intense, rigorous, and is tracked more closely. By sixth or seventh grade, we know if a child has progressed beyond a fourth grade level in the core classes. By ninth and tenth grade, we know if a child is proficient in reading and writing, and is going to be ready for college by graduation. There's a common saying that I believe is completely true. It goes "It's not about how smart you are, it's about how you are smart." Is every child going to be a brilliant brain surgeon, engineer, writer, lawyer, orator, athlete, or any of the other professions we place up on a pedestal? Obviously not. What are we now doing for those who aren't going to be? Precious little. We still force them to take the same courses as their academically proficient counterparts and then push them out the door, horribly unprepared for the professional world.

Look, the world needs people to do menial labor. The world needs people to do the technical jobs. And the world needs people to do those jobs which are so difficult that only the brightest should be placed in them. More and more, there is a growing gap between those who do the highest skilled jobs and those who just find themselves doing menial labor. Hence the diminishing middle class (not entirely the fault of Ford, GM, and Chrysler sending jobs overseas) and the growing "eat the rich" movement. The technical jobs are losing out. Mike Rowe is a prominent advocate for the trades. And he's right, they are in high demand and not being filled. Students who don't excel in academics often become so frustrated with organized learning that by the time they graduate they've written off continued education, not knowing or caring that you don't need six years and a master's degree to be a carpenter, AND to make more money by the end of your training than most of your college-bound counterparts will make in their early and mid-twenties.

Under my system, the eighth, ninth, and tenth grade years will be spent making sure these kids can read and write at an adult level; that is, enough to survive and not be swindled by life. Then, they would spend their time moving into the trades. These would be any job that pays more than menial labor but doesn't require years worth of university study to earn a certification and begin excelling in it. Think about it. What if Sally Doesn'tsitstillinclass and Johnny ADHD and Leroy Lovestoworkwithhishands and Karen Daydreamsanddoodlesallday were placed into programs where they could learn carpentry, plumbing, x rays, anesthesia, fabrication, nurses assistant, any number of kinesthetic arts, culinary, cosmetics/beautician, handyman/remodeling, landscaping, farming, electrical, gardening, mechanics, tool and dye, or any number of trades of this nature, along with taking business classes so they can learn to write their own paycheck in their twenties instead of working dead-end jobs and racking up debt? The working professionals already established in these trades would have the benefit of cheap labor and passing on their skills to the next generation, along with being able to take part in the contributions to society I list in the business section of this book. Kids could spend their high school years learning their trades, working apprenticeships on the job, and enter adulthood leaving the menial labor to younger teenagers, college students, and bored retirees; the people these jobs should really be reserved for. I'm not talking about a couple of semesters in shop classes or a skill center. Those too often have no effect on a child's future, or are seen as blow-off classes. I'm talking about full-on educational paths that lead a child to a brighter future than stocking Walmart shelves. Another benefit of this is that the brilliant kids who spend all of their school day in the academic classes could spend their after-school hours or teenage years following early graduation in the same programs, learning things that will at the very least help them in life, if not even give them another career option. Just because a kid can spend eight years in college doesn't mean they have to. It's no less noble spending your days fixing broken pipes in customer houses than it is to fly a commercial airliner. The only difference is the rate of pay. Too often, the rate of pay argument can't even be applied, as the academically brilliant kids go to college and are swindled into gender studies, comparative dance theory, and other majors of learning that don't render the paychecks but still expect the debt to be repaid.

Make all school curriculum a non-negotiable, and allow students to REALLY do it at their own pace. If we did this and followed through, we may not have to demolish standardized testing, as making every kid learn and complete everything that is on the menu would result in testing scores taking care of themselves. School is not a buffet. I've said this so many times to so many students and yet even the best of them treat school as such. "I'll take this side of roast beef but leave the vegetables" says the kid at the buffet. It's the wrong mentality. As a teacher I've seen far too many kids skip the hardest assignments and projects and do as little as possible to maintain a passing grade. The aforementioned knuckleheads who have poor attendance and even poorer work ethic are worse, as they don't care about maintaining a passing grade. They know summer school and credit recovery are easier options down the road. It's the mentality that disregards investments for the future in lieu of withdrawals for today. Being kids, they don't really understand the long-term ramifications of their choices, as that part of their brain isn't fully developed yet. I've preached until I'm blue in the face that you don't build a house from the roof down, and the earlier assignments they've skipped are the foundation for what we are doing in the present. Schools often say that "failure is not an option" but until they really change their ways, it is an option. So what schools need to do is give them one and only one option. Lock them in a windowless room with no access to the attic and which only has one door. Give them the key to the door and tell them that's the only way out. And mean it when you say it. I'd add to Edward James Olmos words in that I'd say that students will rise to the level of expectations <u>you set and enforce for them</u>. Too often, schools set expectations but don't enforce them. I've already addressed removing summer school and credit recovery options. If we do away with standardized testing (along with the other nonsensical, feel good, self-celebrating, ridiculous interruptions schools engage in), we will have more time in the classroom for what really counts; actual learning.

It must be said because it can't be assumed, that a teacher's yearly curriculum should be under the purview (with administrative review) of said teacher. One problem of the Common Core, Grade Level Content Expectations, and other forms of government oversight give no agency to teachers to run their own classrooms. They actually turn teachers into obedient drones, merely pressing buttons here and there to produce desired and equal results in all students. This is an enemy of true education. Individual schools and teachers should be given the liberty to choose, implement, and enforce their own curricula and entice parents to make the choice to send their students there based on this and other beneficial factors. Quite simply put, I should as a teacher, pick books and resources which fulfill my grade level expectations, hand them out to the students at the beginning of the year, and tell them that they are not going to move on to the next grade's work until they finish all assignments contained herein, and that I'll be at my desk browsing eHarmony profiles should anyone need my help. JK on that last independent clause.

I'm an English teacher. One of the challenges to teaching English is that unlike much of math, social studies, and science, there is not always an objective answer. Until you get into conceptual math, two plus two equals four. Until you start talking about analyzing why an historical event happened, the Declaration of Independence was signed and the Revolutionary War began in 1776. Until you start into theorizing on things which don't satisfy the scientific method (observable, recordable, repeatable), acids and bases cancel each other out. Ask a student what the theme(s) is/are in the book *Of Mice and Men* and you'll get a blank stare. Student's don't like subjective answers. They think there is a right answer to everything, so even the most brilliant avoid venturing a guess on the meaning of that novel. Subjective answers are intimidating when you're used to the right/wrong paradigm. That's why I start with the foundational parts of our language, the often-ignored realm of grammar.

I won't get too much into the Common Core and its shortcomings. That's a topic for its own book. What I will say is that the CC is frustrating for a high school English teacher because it doesn't stress the foundations of our language. There's only one strand devoted to mastery of the language foundations and it's really there to get standardized test questions about parallel structure and subject-verb agreement into the curriculum. When you look at the strands devoted to college-level reading and writing skills, it'd be possible to avoid the grammar strand altogether due to time constraints or whatever excuse you wish to contrive. I attended a private school and I was still pointing out gerunds and diagramming sentences in twelfth grade. Problem is, as I said above, you don't build a house from the roof down. You don't start a race by breaking the tape. You don't cook dinner by taking the chicken off the grill. You don't mainline heroin by first tying off your arm. Pick whatever metaphor you want. Ignoring language foundations so kids can read and write at a college level is downright stupid. Excuse my harsh language. I usually don't get this worked up. Thinking about soft and somewhat runny French Toast and.............we're good.

I see the four main components of an English classroom as grammar, literature, vocabulary acquisition, and writing. Instead of jumping around from component to component, I give them their own block of dedicated time. I start with grammar, move to reading skills, combine literature and vocabulary acquisition, and finish the year with writing. As I mentioned before, I give students much of their work on Schoology. It's a resource that makes my life easier. All objective questions can be answered and graded automatically. Students can see what they got wrong (instantaneous feedback instead of delayed feedback because their teacher has a stack of papers sitting on his desk at home but didn't get to them because the Lions were losing another game) and redo it immediately for a better grade (instead of waiting until they get their paper back when the concept might not be fresh in their minds anymore). Schoology allows me to assign an entire year's sequence of learning and force students to get a passing grade on one assignment before they are allowed to move to the next. This removes the possibility of treating school as a buffet. So then, passing or failing are the only options. If students don't have credit recovery or summer school as an option, the overwhelming majority of them will rise to the level of expectations. Those who don't can take a hike. Sorry, but life is tough. If I can't teach you, then life will teach you. When life teaches you some of its harsh lessons, come talk to me and then we can have a fresh start and do something great together. Forced sequential learning is a beautiful thing. Other sites like Khan Academy, Study Island, and others have similar paradigms. I like Schoology (I use Study Island in the reading skills portion of my learning also) because it allows me to make my own question banks.

Here's where the self-paced learning comes into play. As a teacher I've said many times I should be able to hand a student a grammar book, a writing book, and a literature book at the beginning of the school year and tell them they will pass my class when they are all finished. Same goes for a teacher in the other cores. What makes it easier for them is that their learning can often come from a single textbook, and that learning is sequentially laid out already. I hand my students a grammar book, tell them to read, take notes, learn the first concept, and then go to Schoology to finish the assignment attached to that learning. Seeing the hardworking ones do it on their own is a beautiful thing, as it allows me to engage in small group time with the not-so-hardworking and answer the occasional questions the self-guided kids have. And because I know my students' reading levels, I can accommodate on Schoology with questions that are easier for the lower skilled and special needs students without any other students ever knowing that they are receiving accommodations/modifications. Having them read from a book (I'm still not onboard with the "have them watch a YouTube video to learn how to conjugate a verb" mentality) to learn the concept satisfies my desire to keep things somewhat old school (there's research to support the practice of reading a physical book) while having them do their work digitally (on top of the grading time it saves me) satisfies modern students' desire to

have electronic stimulation (along with the administrators' desire to have 21st century learning happening) and
we all win in the process (enough parenthetical breaks
in one sentence for you?).

And now, here's the rub. We have one-hundred-
eighty school days in a year. If every teacher across
the land made their entire curriculum a non-negotiable and were supported in this measure by admin-
istration, many students will need every second of
those one-hundred-eighty days (maybe more) to finish their year's worth of work. I call this Year-to-Year
Accountability (trademark pending, but not really).
However, many brilliant students will finish quite
early. They'll work on their weekday evenings, Friday
nights, Saturday mornings, Sunday afternoons, and
holiday breaks to finish early. Come March, April, and
even February of that school year, many of them will
be finishing that year's work. Instead of sitting and
waiting for the teacher to control the knuckleheads
and silently laughing at the learning time that's being wasted, they will be plugging away, making investments for the future. What do we do with them
then? Simple, we give them the next year's work.
Why should a kid who finishes early not be given
the chance to go on to the next grade? Or, reward
them by saving all of the field trips (both academic
and fun-based) and job shadowing for the end of the
year when the warmth and nice weather makes them
more enjoyable and safer anyway. They can come to

school each day knowing they'll be going somewhere and doing something fun. Removing an ever-growing chunk of kids from campus for the day will reduce distractions for the strugglers while also providing them an incentive to finish things up (and making classroom management much easier for the teachers who stay on campus). We educators talk about self-paced learning and individualized learning plans. More often than not, it's just an epithet for slowing down to keep to the struggling students in the game. It does a horrible disservice to those who don't struggle. If they were allowed to finish at their own pace, we'd see a whole spate of kids graduating high school at ages twelve, thirteen, fourteen, and so on. What then? Well then we put them in the trades programs I've discussed above, the menial labor workforce to save up for college, or early entrance into college for those whose parents can afford it or those who are given scholarships. The options aren't limited at all. Doogie Howser, while a fictional character, was a wonderful example of what we'd see, and not even close to being farfetched. I yearn for the days when Iron Man's flying techno battle suit of awesomeness isn't all that farfetched but it probably won't happen until I'm old and worn down.

What do we do with those who struggle? Well, their self-paced learning will often lead into the summer just because of their struggles, but they will start feeling the pinch around April and May, know that they won't be given the option of summer school, and start to buckle down. If they graduate high school at age seventeen, eighteen, or even beyond that, so be it. At least they did it. Having a slower entrance into adulthood doesn't mean it's ruined for them. It does no good to push them through in the name of curbing rates of retention. We did our part in forcing them to do theirs. In turn, this will lead, in about a generation, to the most skilled and naturally hardworking group of young adults we've ever had in this country. The drops in crime, teenage pregnancy, underage substance abuse (kids can't debauch themselves with their nose in a book), depression/suicide (people are less depressed when they have a goal and purpose and work is the best form of those), and government dependency will all be icing on the cake.

Private Property

WE HAVE A problem with private property in this country. It's the driving force in our economy, and upholding the concept of individual/agreed upon group ownership is how transactions are made. Honest men cannot engage in trade with one another if you cannot make a legitimate claim of ownership to your house, stuff, time, services, and children (just kidding, but not really, but really am, but really not at all, but really totally am, he loves me, he loves me not). But we have limited private property, not free of outside influence, not free to disperse or use as we see fit, and not free of government encroachment. Here's what we need to do:

Change the way we view property that isn't doing anything right now. It's no secret those who own land do better in this country. For a stark comparison, look at those Native American tribes who own their land as compared to those who stay on reservations the government oversees and controls. It's no competition. Those who are free to work, cultivate, and disperse their land as they see fit prosper vastly better than those who are given casinos and not much else.

Same goes for the rest of the country. I tell my students and children and any young person who will listen to me that they should rent in their early twenties and wait until they can pay cash for land or build a house on their own. I think the housing crash in the time of Obama shows that mortgages in your financially unstable twenties are not the way to go. Your twenties should be spent acquiring college/trade and work experience, living cheaply, stockpiling cash, investing in the stock market, starting small business, and avoiding loans as much as possible. But when you're ready, the acquisition and development of land is a way to get ahead and set your future self up for comfort and ease of living. Once again, look at blacks in this country. Black Americans own the funniest videos on the internet and not much else. Precious few own and operate prime real estate in bustling metropolises. When it comes to dying metropolises, I'd see no problem at all handing over commercial and residential property to the black folk who already dominate the population in large cities. This would allow them to change these places from the inside out. I have a dream someday of acquiring commercial property here in Flint, allowing blacks to open and operate small businesses in them, and giving them a contractual arrangement favorable to them in times of plenty and in times of...the opposite of plenty. Dearth,

I think the word would be. Maybe Dearth Vader is the word. I conflate reality and fiction sometimes. It goes like this:

I own a piece of commercial property in a majority black area of Flint. A black prospective business owner comes to me with a proposal of opening a small business in it. They can choose to buy with a normal monthly payment over time, or rent so long as they occupy it. If they choose the first option and their business fails, or grows to the point where they want to relocate and don't want to shoulder the burden of ownership, I retain ownership of the property and chalk what they've paid so far up to rent and repeat the process with someone else. If they choose the second option and they succeed in business, thereby helping the community around them, I give them an option to buy, and use an agreed upon percentage of their rent up to that point as collateral toward ownership. This is a common practice for mobile home parks, but not in commercial properties. Either way, it's low-risk for both parties and would bring more businesses than dollar stores, liquor stores, and pawn stores to black-dominated neighborhoods. Or, we could circumvent this whole process and have commercial and residential properties in dying metropolises handed over to the people who live and work in these metropolises with the proviso (and offer to help) that they need to do something with it within a certain timeframe. I don't have a problem with the government doing this as much blighted land in my city is owned by the government-run land bank anyway. The local government in my city has devoted some of their time to tearing down blighted housing but allocated much more time and money to building affordable housing. With the help of new private owners who know they will forfeit their claim if they dawdle, measures like removing and replacing blight will giddy up faster.

This is where conservatives jump in and talk about crime rates in black neighborhoods impeding businesses. With my ideas for reducing crime, changing prisons, giving reparations, and bettering education, this argument should eventually become moot. So, as soon as Jay-Z, the mucky-mucks at Disney, Mark Zuckerberg, Bill Gates, Elon Musk, Robert Downey Jr, Kevin Hart, the king of Jordan, the fictional characters from Crazy Rich Asians, and Scrooge McDuck can find the time checking under their couch cushions for loose change and scrounge up a $20 million donation for my Save-the-City-of-Flint Foundation, I'll be ready to use my foundation to save the city of Flint and make our success the blueprint for other impoverished cities not so fortunate to have a guy like me around.

I estimate that's a good ballpark figure for what it would take to completely turn around the city's blight, acquire and renovate all of the abandoned housing just sitting in the land bank, fix up and beautify the properties of those who cannot afford it, open small businesses in the stagnant and boarded commercial properties peppering the area, and push the slumlords out, or at least apply pressure for them to better their ways. Now, if I had $100 million, I'd not only save the city but ensure its survival and combat the inevitable atrophying that happens when a good deed isn't backed by the flow of money and responsible choices. I'd open an automobile manufacturing facility and provide the city's young people looking to start their professional lives according to my paradigm above, which should be more than enough to keep the UAW leeches at bay (they aren't entirely to blame for Flint's job market demise, but they are not entirely blameless). But hey, I'm just a guy sitting in front of his computer ini boxer briefs and a not-so-white-anymore undershirt trying to think of ways to help folks.

Beyond that, we could solve our homeless problem with private property. Using my model for companies paying for postsecondary training and education for young people, we could do the same for homeless people. There are exceptions to the rule, but many homeless folk became that way through bad life choices, often involving substance abuse. I'd say companies could start acquiring residential and commercial properties all over the place (or cultivate business relationships with local landlords), then hire those who are in the valleys of life to work at their places of business in exchange for room, board, and transportation to and from work. Money doesn't need to change hands, giving these folks a chance to straighten out their lives without the temptation of using a regular paycheck to make irresponsible choices. United Plastics; a company founded by David Kaufman (a wonderful man and longtime friend who is now deceased) here in Flint did just that for people needing a job as they were recovering from substance abuse and couldn't find gainful employment elsewhere due to less than sterling work and legal records. David's company operated this way because he was a recovering cocaine addict himself. He had been afforded more second chances than he could count and wanted to do the same for others. Will there be some failures, setbacks, and frauds? Of course. But there will also be successes. Furthermore, companies could compete for the best and most dedicated workers by offering the health, dental, and vision care so many of the homeless sorely need. I don't advocate living like this the rest of your life, as we should always be improving our life, selves, and station, but it would be a vital stepping stone these folks need, and add to the solution our current minimum wage debate presents.

Change what people are allowed do on private property. Here's a fix to the water crisis we face in Flint and other communities. Stop giving people only one option for water. The government, as has been shown time and time again, is really bad at handling things when they have no competition. I remember vividly in 2016, my mother called me up and told me to not drink the water and not allow my children to drink the water. The very next morning, Flint got about eight inches of snow. The conservative and old-school side of me said that I should go out into the yard, collect snow in any receptacle I can find, boil it down, then fill and stockpile water jugs with it. The entitled American side of me said that I shouldn't have to do that. Now, imagine a Native American or frontiersman living with that type of entitlement. "Living" being the operative word, as it's something they wouldn't do for very long. The government and various charitable agencies like local churches started handing out bottled water, but this was just a band-aid on the symptom, not a cure because it didn't ask the people to take measures to be self-sufficient. Instead of shunting resources to these efforts, the government could pay contractors to dig holes in properties, install wells and collection, filtration, and pumping systems (when's the last time you saw a cistern in the basement of a recently built house?). Once the city of Flint is updated in this manner, they could encourage the same efforts in other places. This would allow well, rain, and snow water to be used instead of government-provided water, thereby giving the government water agency competition, thereby giving them a reason to get their act together. It would also reduce the population's water bills and result in lower government dependency among the American people; always a good thing.

Yes, water collection and filtration systems would increase electric bills. Once more, government can do something about this, something that reduces, you guessed it, government dependency. It's no secret, even for someone who has skipped certain sections of this book, that we have a welfare issue in this country. It's not uncommon for the government to pay the energy bills of those receiving assistance. There's a fix-in-waiting, just waiting to be implemented by a square-jawed alpha male who regularly gives up his weekends to do volunteer work. Just Google "Solar Freakin' Roadways" and you'll be introduced to the novel (some might say revolutionary, and yes, I've legally changed my name to "some") idea of replacing our asphalt, brick, and concrete roads with durable glass solar panels. They prognosticate that if the entire country were to do this with roads, driveways, and parking lots, they could power the United States for two years with one year's worth of sunlight collection. I am sure our federal government, with the power it wields, could come to some deal with companies like this one, to supply free or reduced electricity to the population in exchange for a sweet, sweet government contract. I am a fan of small government, but like the Federalists I am also a fan of strong government. This would give people another option outside of traditional gas and electric corporations for their energy needs, and give the Democrats pining for clean, renewable energy something to write home to ma about. It would also remove the need for Tony Stark to surrender his arc reactor technology, thereby giving him the chance to continue fighting intergalactic crime free of summons to testify in front of a congressional oversight committee headed by a secretly villainous Gary Shandling (RIP). Solar Freakin' Roadways also promise expanded access to water from rain and snowfall, thereby giving the government more competition, thereby giving them all the more reason to get their act together, and reducing government dependency in this country, which I think I've mentioned before, is a good thing. Forgive me for being redundant. Forgive me for being redundant.

We have a problem with waste in this country, and getting people to separate their garbage and go out of their way to recycle is a lot to ask. Landfills are eyesores and some argue that they poison the ground. If you have been in the basement of many houses built eighty to a hundred years ago, you might have noticed coal shoots and incinerators. Go back a few decades, and you'll see that people used wood stoves to cook their foods. Increased comfort standards in our country have increased our dependency on natural gas and therefore, government regulated industries and services. Were I president, I'd pay contractors to install incinerators in homes and businesses again. This would allow people to heat and store energy in their homes by burning combustible waste like paper, cardboard, clothing, wood, dryer lint, Styrofoam, the bodies of their enemies, and so on. The idea of painted and dyed combustibles hurting the ozone could be fixed by simply compelling the companies to stop coating them with dyes, chemicals, and paints that are harmful when burnt. Revolutionary ideas, remember? Just because it's hard doesn't make it impossible. Humans (of which I believe many corporations are still made up of) are wonderfully adaptable creatures. Arguably, more adaptable because their ability to make profits often depends on them being their best selves due to competition from competing competitors. When it comes to humans who burn things that are harmful, emission detection and measurement systems can be installed on these in order to keep people accountable for burning only what should be burnt. Furthermore, I believe the opportunity for someone who can make a hybrid stove that both cooks food and heats a house (like they used to), and which runs on natural gas, solar power, electricity, propane, wood, grease, pedal power (see *Omega Man*), and adorable hamsters running in a wheel, is just sitting there. Making and selling such a stove would allow those of us who don't mind trading a little extra effort in wood collection in order to save money on gas and electricity. My parents still burn wood for heat in the winter, and their Consumers Power bill is laughably low. Once again, this reduces gov...you know the rest.

We have a problem with plastic waste in this country, and efforts to recycle and reuse plastic hasn't made much of a dent in it. I think we will come to the point that a complete moratorium on the production and distribution of plastic goods will eventually be imposed by a bold leader, if not the mandate to produce plastic from biodegradable hemp. That will make Woody Harrelson and all the stoners in your life happy. The conservative side of me says that government should not meddle in business like this, but the liberal side of me forces me to recognize the aftereffects on our bodies of water and the wildlife trying to live there. Short of dumping all our plastic waste in the Sahara Desert, I don't see an easy way out of this. Once again, government can step in and save us from our consumptionist ways. 3-D printers have become popular in recent years, and are commonly used to make things that are useful in everyday lives. Plastic melts at a much lower temperature than metal and steel, so basements and utility rooms should be equipped with devices for such a task. The government that distributes a combination plastic melting and 3-D printing system would allow people to recycle their plastics and make useful things out of them would be genius in reducing our national waste problem. Maybe even set a good example for those countries that are blatantly careless in terms of polluting their waters with plastic waste (cough cough, China, cough). Guys, seriously, if I end up dead upon the publishing of this book, you know where to start looking.

After this, what would Americans be throwing away? Mostly food waste and metal. Food waste can be used in so many different ways, as it's organic material that can be used to help the earth and those living in it. Here in Michigan, we have a rescue bear farm that collects food waste from local restaurants.

Watching the bears come and eat their slop is just part of the charm of this absolutely adorable tourist attraction, tucked away in that little, secret country we Michiganders refer to as the Upper Peninsula. I went there and was able to hug and get my picture taken with a bear cub as it enthusiastically munched on Froot Loops the caretaker placed on its belly. One of the fondest memories I've ever logged. Add me as a friend on Facebook, dig through my old posts, and you'll be able to see a poor quality video shot during the infancy of smartphones of this event. I can't remember many happier moments of my life than the one in which I got to hug and feed a baby bear loudly cooing for more Fruit Loops. Feeding rescued bears is just one smart way we could do about our food waste. What if our government taught people how to and facilitated the practice of growing their own food on their own land? It's the teach-a-gender-fluid-carbon-unit-to-fish paradigm. This would give people the incentive to compost and use food waste to make more food. It would also reduce consumption of fast food; always a good thing.

Moving on. Metal is easily recycled, and quite valuable to those engaged in its recycling, thereby conferring value to those willing to take it to be recycled. To sum it up, government already picks winners when they give contracts out or provide services that they own exclusively. Government isn't in the business of fixing things long term though. If they picked the winners giving people the ability to live more efficient and less wasteful lives, they'd be giving long term solutions to some of the issues our children's children will face.

Beyond this, landowners face the issue of updating, renovating, or building on their land only at the behest of government. In big cities, ordinances disallow people from burning on their property due to the close proximity of neighbors and the public safety risk it poses. Beyond that, I am of the mind that government should get out of policing private property. There are people who have done prison sentences for building windmills and porches on their property without government permission. This smacks of blatant overreach. If I want to install a windmill, solar panels, or a deck on my house, I should be allowed to do so. This is a day and age when we, as informed consumers, are able to find reputable contractors to do quality work on our properties without much effort. Those who can't afford reputable contractors but don't want shoddy work on their property can just, you know, forego any changes they want to do, or learn to do it themselves. Were my paradigm for schools adopted, the next generation of students will be well-versed in the handsy skills so much more common to generations gone by anyway. Where, beyond electric, carpentry, masonry, and plumbing codes, does government need to be a part of this process, beyond the desire to add unnecessary bureaucracy to the process?

Set up schools as land proprietors. It's common

enough for schools to service families which qualify under the law as homeless. School attendance and achievement in the classroom is made exponentially more difficult for a child in this situation. Schools can ease this suffering by having readily available housing to fill such needs without having to rely on inter-governmental program support (often the opposite of expedient) in order to place and prosper these families.

What's more, if schools owned, operated, sold, and rented local housing, apartment complexes, and businesses, they could alleviate budget concerns with added revenue streams, provided the handling of said revenue was in the hands of ethical persons, not the clutches of the villainous and opportunistic. On top of that, it would give the schools a vested interest in keeping the communities they serve clean, safe, and on the upkeep. Lastly, it would give their secondary students valuable experience in all matters related to housing, like maintaining cleanliness and making repairs, along with providing them with employment opportunities in close cooperation with their schools, employment which they can use toward my paradigm of labor force overhaul and college tuition payment. All of these would greatly benefit rural and urban districts, where blight and substandard housing are a bigger problem and impediment to school success than in suburban districts. Not to mention the chance for teachers in need of supplemental income to spend part time hours working close to the school operating and managing said businesses and housing concerns. I see wins all around. Do you? I mean, it's cool if you don't. I'm not here to please everybody, but it sure would be a blow to my crippling social anxiety if I *could* please everybody.

Stop stealing private property! Easier said than done, I know. Most of the ideas I've come up with in this ever increasingly tedious ramble are of the practical sort. This is, however, an appeal to the moral. I don't know if private property is sacred, but we could surely fix a multitude of problems in this country if every person treated it as such. Were I president, I'd start my first year by asking every American to resolve to spend that year treating the property of every other man as off-limits. Roll your eyes if you want, but the president has a lot of influence over the minds, attitudes, and even actions of a lot of citizens. If American citizens were given incentives like tax breaks to abide by the law, and collectively decided that we weren't going to steal anymore, a lot of suffering would vanish. We wouldn't have to lock our doors and cars anymore, nor buy expensive alarm systems and loss-related insurance policies. The need for interactions involving violent force and guns would plummet. The poor can disown the perversion of the Robin Hood ethic that stealing from the American rich is okay because it's not a big hit to them. The poor can stop holding down the rest of the poor by not stealing from each other anymore (a much bigger problem in large urban centers than the poor stealing from the rich). With my proposed change in businesses all around, so amply elucidated above, the poor can also stop arguing about how the rich steal from them in terms of unlivable minimum wage. This is a win-win-win-win-win-win-win-win-win-win-win-win- repeated 350 million times.

Philosophy

CHANGE THE PHILOSOPHY of how we view each other. Too many of those on the political right view discourse, political action, public law, policy, etc. in terms of winning and losing. Too many on the political left certainly do the same ("Eat the rich", anyone?). Libertarians frame themselves in opposition to both sides. Facebook and cable news have made the aggressive contrarian posing even worse. What we don't understand when we do this, beyond the destructive and divisive nature of such ranting, is that it's not really the truth. We aren't in a competition to win this country. The people we oppose in the public forum are those same people serving us food, healing our wounds, mowing our yards, teaching our kids, answering our complaints, petting our dog as we cross paths in the park, and even sitting next to us in our respective religious ceremonies. America really is unique in all the world, it's present and past. We are a nation of honest men engaging in trade with each other, no matter the divergent backgrounds and worldviews we hail from. Thomas Paine wouldn't be spinning in his grave if he could see us today. Thieves, liars, the corrupt, warmongers, philanderers, fanatics, adulterers, lunatics, murderers, rapists, and pederasts existed long before and during his day, no matter the nostalgic and somewhat disingenuous pining for the good ole' days Republicans love to do. He could see what this burgeoning land was becoming and what it promised to become, in spite of the wickedness that lurks in the hearts of men. If he could see us today, he'd probably be so happy he'd slam dunk an alley-oop from John Stockton over the sizable hands of Patrick Ewing. Not sure if you know, but that complicated fanciful sequence is the scientific opposite of spinning in your grave.

We aren't in this to win something politically and make the other side lose. I want the careers, family lives, personal emotional journeys, and Florida vacations of those who see God and the world differently than me to go swimmingly. I don't despise anyone for thinking, believing, and acting differently than me. Individual soul liberty mandates I enjoy my own autonomy without begrudging the next guy his own. This "those whom I've labeled in opposition to me don't get free speech on my page. BLOCKED!" mentality will take nobody nowhere no-how, no what I mean? The first presidential candidate who comes along, says, means, and actually acts upon a real and genuine philosophy of unity will have my vote, and probably those of most of the country.

Conclusion

MY BOOK HAS concluded.

Closing Thoughts

I'VE PROMISED CHANGE and I'm going to deliver it. Do you think we can do it? I think we can. Scratch that, I know we can. I believe in us. Ready? Go wolfpack on three! "1-2-3, Gooooooooooooo Wolfpack!"

A Nate Roberts Joint